Random Thoughts of a STUPID MAN

By
Mike Turnbull

Rivershore Books
Cover design by Kiernan Manion
Cover photo by Mike Flaten
Author photo courtesy of author

ISBN-13: 978-0615972398
ISBN-10: 061597239X
First published in 2012

PRINTED IN THE UNITED STATES OF AMERICA

This book is dedicated to my dad, Jack Turnbull. He is the original "Stupid Man" in my family. I know this because I heard both my grandma and my mom call him a "Stupid Man" at various times in my life. He died way too young. I know I would have been a lot smarter if we would have had more years together. I know he still watches over me, and I hope he feels some sense of pride in how my life has turned out so far, and is happy with how I have carried the torch for "Stupid Men." If there is a "Stupid Man" club in heaven, I hope they let me in, when and if I get there.

REVIEWS

"Way cool! Who knew you could even compose a complete sentence? Want to come and give an author talk some day on campus? I'd buy you lunch and cover your mileage even... Seriously!" - Kelly McCalla

"Thanks so much for the pleasurable reading experience. Also, for the kind words written about myself and Anna." - Gerry Levos

"I just finished Stupid Man this morning. I identified with everything in there and enjoyed every page. I realized for certain that I am also not so bright. It just doesn't hurt so much knowing I'm not the only one." - Paul Grove

"Outstanding! I always thought men were pigs...but maybe they are just stupid." - Dan Skogen

"Each year, I try to find something that is unique and interesting for my wife Jean to make Christmas a little more interesting. I discovered that a former colleague, who was an outstanding educator and coach, is now an accomplished author. Congratulations!" - Terry Teiken

"You beautiful man... Congrats on this achievement. Writing a book is a real life changer in many ways. For some reason people think you are a lot smarter than you actually are. I'm proud of you Turny...you always were a cerebral cat; awesome!" - Ed Nordskog

"I just finished your book and wanted to thank you for writing it! I laughed, teared up, nodded my head in agreement, and was given a whole new view of you and your stories. I appreciate you taking the time to share your stories. I am blessed to know you." - Shelly Flaten

REVIEWS

CONTENTS

PREFACE

Today is Thursday, June 16, 2011, and I am beginning to write a book. The first question is why? That one is easy: I told some people in my life that I was going to write a book this summer. I usually don't go public so boldly with thoughts unless I plan on getting it done. So, now that the promise is out there, today I'm officially starting. I've been thinking about writing a book for years. I actually started out as an English major at Vermilion Community College in Ely, Minnesota in 1977. I developed a passion—I don't claim skill or a knack, just a passion for writing, and that passion was fueled by my instructor, Nadine Marsnik. The original plan was to be a high school English teacher and coach. I eventually was talked out of the English teaching thing by people who told me coaching would take up so much of my time and energy that I wouldn't want to be up late correcting papers. I still have not lost the passion for writing, and we'll all know whether or not I have the skill when I'm done writing this book.

RANDOM THOUGHT NUMBER ONE

On occasion I wear a t-shirt that reads across the chest: "Have you ever stopped to think and just not started again?"

I am 52 years old and have been married to my wife, Pam, for 29 years. We have a daughter who is married and living in Nebraska and a son living and working in Minneapolis, Minnesota. I have taught and coached throughout the state of Minnesota for 30 years. I spent the first 12 years of my career at the high school level and the last 18 at the college level. I have a bachelor's degree in social studies education and a master's degree in sport's management. All this said; I'm pretty sure I get called a "Stupid Man" at least once a day, and if not by someone else, I usually catch me mumbling it to myself. Most of the time my wife is the one who points it out, sometimes with a loving tone in her voice and at times with an air of disbelief. My daughter, mother, athletic trainer, sisters, players I coach (women's volleyball and basketball), and on a rare occasion my mother-in-law have been able to chime in. I love and respect all these women in my life and thank them for pointing out the flawed, "Stupid Man" that I am. I have learned to respect the opinions of others, but like any other person with enough experience, education, and limited wisdom, I'm in there, battling and muddling my way through life every day.

RANDOM THOUGHT NUMBER TWO

Tomorrow I am driving to Omaha, Nebraska, to watch the College Baseball World Series. This will be the fourth time I've been there. It is truly the "Greatest Show on Dirt!" One of my favorite reasons for going is that my daughter and son-in-law live in Nebraska. I was there for the final go at Rosenblatt Stadium last year, and I'm looking forward to seeing TD Ameritrade Park. Sad to see all the tradition of Rosenblatt go away, but I'm sure the CWS will continue to thrive.

Back to writing this book—I plan to attempt to take you on a journey throughout my life and the world as I know it, for what it is worth. As in my life, I'm not really sure where we are going, but each day is part of the puzzle and eventually, with the help of others, it will be finished. I want my friends and relatives to rest assured that I did write this, and I did type the original copy on a computer. For those of you who don't know, this spring I began typing my own stuff, and I'm actually beginning to use my left hand and incorporate a second and third finger into the process. Carpal tunnel is not something I fear.

RANDOM THOUGHT NUMBER THREE

Kristin and Steph, thanks for introducing me to the glorious world of the "right click." I don't dabble in it very often, but it is interesting to see what that side of the mouse can do.

If you do decide to go ahead and read this book, please keep in mind that all stories and accounts are as I remember them. Some, I'm sure are right on the money, some are probably tainted, but this is how I've etched them in my memories over time. Either way, I hope you enjoy.

FOREWORD

By Dr. Trent Janezich

I have known Mike Turnbull for the most transformational thirteen years of my life. Granted, I am only 31, so there really aren't that many periods of thirteen years to go on, but nevertheless, you get my point. Over the course of these thirteen years, I have been Coach's student, player, and most recently his colleague, but always his friend. Who knows, one day if he hangs around long enough, I may even be his boss. I think he will retire before that has a chance of happening

When Coach told me he was writing a book I thought three things. First, I wondered if he was going to handwrite it like he wrote a letter of recommendation for me once; second, I was wondering when and how he managed to learn to use the computer; and third, I was slightly envious and proud of him because everyone at one stage of their life or another thinks about writing a book, but they usually don't get around to actually doing it. After I got over the shock and after we discussed his concept, I said jokingly, "Hey, if you need someone to write the foreword for you, let me know." At some point he determined that this was a good idea, so here I am.

I made the determination that it would probably be good if I had a couple of my teammates add their thoughts about Coach as well. One of my teammates, Travis MacLeod, said of Coach:

> Coach Turnbull is one of the more unique, caring, and hard-working guys I've ever met. My favorite memories from Coach come from riding shotgun while he was driving the van on long road trips, how he would handwrite everything (until this book, apparently), all of his crazy stories, it becoming clear that he never sleeps (mostly because he constantly had a Mountain Dew in hand), and most of all listening to his knowledge on the game, girls, and life. In the two years I played for him, it was clear he would do anything for his players (except bail them out of jail), and he is one of the people I can thank for helping to get me where I'm at today.

If you were to take a poll of all of his players, my guess is a great majority would say the same as Travis. One of my roommates during my time at Hibbing Community College was Ryan Lee. Ryan and I came to Hibbing Community College together from Fridley, Minnesota. Ryan described Coach Turnbull as a "father figure, someone you could always talk to about anything—he always had a great sense of humor and was a great teacher on and off the court." I think it is safe to say that when Coach's former players get together and reminisce about the "good old days" at Hibbing Community College, we all laugh and have fun at the thought of what was, and we all agree we came away from the experience as better people.

Coach Turnbull's teams were not the best teams in the world. Coach tried to recruit locally and continue the tradition of allowing community college basketball to be truly a "community" college basketball program. He worked with the hand he was dealt more often than not and was worried less about results on the court and more about outcomes of being a student-athlete off the court. Oftentimes our teams would pull off an upset that would make our season, or we would make it to the state tournament and be "competitive enough" because, let's face it, the mission of Division III community college basketball is and should be more than creating the best basketball program in the country. I identified with this because I never played high school basketball and wasn't planning on playing at all at Hibbing Community College. Coach, however, convinced me to play, and while I played sparingly for two seasons, it was the best two years of my college career because of the people and the relationships that were formed through Coach's program.

While I can continue to reminisce about my time and my fellow men's basketball players' experiences with Coach Turnbull, I would be ignoring Coach's interactions with his volleyball and women's basketball players. It would also be interesting to hear what women think about this "Stupid Man."

Lindsay Jacobson, one of Coach's players, said, "I have many stories about Coach Turnbull that may only be funny to the people involved, but what stands out as most important is that Coach made every team a family." He does this by caring for his players and students. Lindsay told me the story about one time when coach cared for her when she was sick:

> We were at Northland Community College playing

> a basketball game, and I got sick at halftime. I had to run off the court before the start of the second half. I was sick for the rest of the half and the whole boys' game. Coach had one of the girls check on me every so often because he couldn't go into the ladies' restroom. Finally, when I could stand up, he walked me to Northland's athletic director's office where I was able to get dressed. He bought me a Sierra Mist and some saltines. These probably ended up hurting me more, since later I found out that I was so sick because I had developed celiac disease (wheat gluten allergy), but it's the thought that counts the most.

Who ever said chivalry was dead? Lindsay also told two other stories about the ways Coach found his way into the hearts of his players:

> The fall of my freshman year, a volleyball teammate of mine and I took an acting class. One night we went with Coach to Itasca Community College to scout a game. On the way home we practiced our monologues for Coach. He was good enough not to laugh and gave us really good feedback. Who knew Coach Turnbull would be so into acting! Coach Turnbull also owns a bed and breakfast, and every winter they have tea parties. He invited his basketball girls to come over for a tea party. It was something different that most people don't get to experience. Coach brings a lot of that to the team. He took us to a potato festival on the way to a volleyball tournament each year; we also went to a statue garden.

Every team that ever played for coach has weird, quirky stories like this. These types of activities are done with purpose, to develop the team's chemistry and the trust between a coach and player. I know the men's basketball or baseball teams never got an invite to the tea parties that Lindsay mentioned were going on at Coach's house (which is probably by design, but nevertheless, I feel slighted in some small way).

Finally, to get the best sense of who Coach Turnbull is, you have to step inside Coach's office. It quite literally is the gateway to his mind, which is proving to be quite organized given his ability to write this book, but which is ironic because his office is a complete mess. He has collages on every wall, with hundreds of pictures of days and players gone by squeezed into poster-style picture frames. These collages are his way of remembering how far he has come and all the players and students he has worked with throughout his career. There are pictures of his younger days, when he didn't have any gray hair, playing baseball at Bemidji State University. You see pictures of his wife, Pam, and his kids, Blaine and Lexie. There are pictures of some of his favorite coaches, like Dean Smith and John Wooden, and books about coaching and life. With each picture, he has at least ten stories to support it. His office is just a disaster. I can't understate this, but for some reason coaches get away with this, and it is viewed as endearing or people coo at the sight of it as if they just saw a little puppy.

I know every time that I walk in there, I feel as if I am in a time portal with my old coach surrounded by old pictures and old memorabilia. It used to be a safe place when I was a student-athlete—a place to banter, to joke, to throw out ideas, to laugh, to talk about successes and failures, to talk about life, family, and love, a place in some cases to be reprimanded, and a place to learn and grow. It is still that way today. As a married adult with two young children, it is still a safe place for me to go to learn, to discuss my career, his career, and our families, and a place where I can air my grievances with the world to someone who will actually listen while withholding judgment. The office is in disarray despite the person he is, and that has its charm, but the office is safe and inviting because of the person he is.

Jenna Zmyslony, another one of coach's student-athletes, had this to say about Coach Turnbull:

> He is probably one of the most brilliant people I have ever met. He seems to know exactly what to say, how to say it, when, and how to hit you across the face with it so you have to deal with it head on. I feel he always knows how to make an impact. He seems more conscious of his words than most, and it makes me wonder how smart he really is. How much of his mind does he actually let across to everyone else?

Mike Turnbull has lived and traveled all over the country and has stories that cut across every slice of Americana for almost every single topic imaginable. His teams took on his personality—less style and more substance. He is quiet, unassuming, and exceptionally insightful, which is why, as has been implied, the title of his book is the most ironic title of all.

CHAPTER ONE

WHERE ARE YOU FROM?

It has always been interesting for me to answer the questions *Where are you from?* or *Where did you grow up?* I'll come back to the first question, but as far as the second, I'm not done growing up, out, old, or any other way, so we'll leave that for someone to answer in my obituary.

RANDOM THOUGHT NUMBER FOUR

I want to be cremated when I die. One of the places I want my ashes scattered is on the pitcher's mound at the Ely Memorial Baseball Field. Standing on top of a pitcher's mound is somewhere I always felt comfortable and in control, from the time I first pitched when I was eight to the last game I pitched at 38 years old. I was blessed enough to play baseball that long and on both coasts and in the Midwest. I have coached baseball most of my adult life. I wouldn't trade back one minute of my life spent on a baseball field.

My dad was a career Navy man, so we lived in a lot of different places during my childhood. I was born in Chester, Pennsylvania, outside of Philadelphia, in 1959 in a hospital that has become, as of the last time I knew, a Planned Parenthood or abortion clinic. I was once also told it was the same hospital in which Jim Croce, the late singer/songwriter, was born.

Not part of my childhood memories, but I believe we did stints in Buhl, Minnesota; Hutchinson, Kansas; somewhere in Tennessee; and Newport, RI. I have two vivid pre-school memories. One, I remember watching *Sally Star*, a TV cowgirl who hosted an afternoon cartoon show in Philadelphia, that showed a lot of *Popeye* and *Tom Terrific*. I also remember John F. Kennedy's assassination, mostly the funeral. I remember hearing my mom and aunt crying in the kitchen over his death. I also remember not being able to watch *Sally Star*, because the funeral broadcast bumped her off the air for what seemed to be days. Don't judge me—I was four and I'm sure showing early indications of being a "Stupid Man."

Kindergarten was spent at a Catholic school in the Philadelphia area. I have memories of one nun who I remember as a very strict disciplinarian. I recall standing on tiptoes to keep my nose on the blackboard and kneeling on wooden rulers, for reasons that seem to have evaded me over the years. First grade was a whirlwind tour. It started in Illinois when my dad was training at Great Lakes Naval Air Station outside of Chicago. Next came two more schools in the Philadelphia area. I remember places called Ridley Park and Toby Farms where we lived, and I'm guessing this spilled into second grade. Now I know this is when the serious groundwork began being laid for my future as a "Stupid Man." I remember these things vaguely: chasing after the ice cream truck that would come through the neighborhood in the evening and watching my uncle, seven years my elder, ride a bike down the street with no hands and eyes closed and then making a very bad attempt at it myself. I'm pretty sure that is the scar on the inside of my left knee. I remember a guy pulling up to the house in a taxi, getting out, talking to my mom, and leaving a hockey stick. Apparently, he played for the Toronto Maple Leafs and was in town to play the Flyers. He was sitting in his hotel room, found our name in the phone book, and came out to see us. We shared the same last name, but apparently that was the only connection.

I also remember the introduction of color television. We didn't have one at the time, but our neighbors did. It was a weekly treat to go over to my friend's house to watch *Batman*. To this day I couldn't tell you what was more thrilling: catching up to the ice cream truck or watching Batman in living color. I got excited just seeing the NBC peacock. One other thing that I'm guessing played into the development of the "Stupid Man" was the mosquito spray truck. There was a truck that would come through our neighborhood every now and then and spray in the sewers, ditches, and creek beds to kill mosquitoes. We would chase after that truck, too. I remember liking the smell. We would also check the sewer tunnels afterwards because rats were easier to catch after the sprayer had been through. Mom, if you are reading this, I blame Dad. I don't know how many times I heard him tell childhood stories of him and his friends catching rats and selling the tails. I will tell you though, we rarely caught one and we had no idea how to get the tails off. I don't seem to be showing any ailments related to this other than being a "Stupid Man," but I'm sure that mosquito spray was probably heavy on DDT.

RANDOM THOUGHT NUMBER FIVE

I trapped another squirrel today. That makes 10 since this spring. I trap them live, drive them out of town, and let them go. They, like me, are a sucker for a peanut butter sandwich. It makes me feel like I'm protecting our home. They chewed holes in our eaves a couple of years ago and nested. Plus, it is always an ego boost to win any battle with a squirrel.

Sometime during second grade we moved to upstate New York. My dad was stationed at a naval air station in Utica. We lived in a little town called Saquoit. We lived in New York long enough for me to finish my fourth grade year. They were great years. Mrs. Davies, my reading teacher in second grade, gave me a Hickory bow and arrow set when I completed the second grade reading curriculum and was able to move on to third grade. She was a savior; I had come in behind and she helped me catch up. Today, I guess they'd call it "No Child Left Behind." Third grade, I had my first teacher crushes, on Miss Lorenzo and her friend, Miss Campbell. Miss Lorenzo broke my heart sometime during the year and got married. So much for no child left behind. In fourth grade, I had my first male teacher, Mr. Lorenti. In fourth grade I also had my first girlfriend, Sally. I can't remember her last name, but her mom packed a great lunch and she would often share. Not so stupid then, was I?

Outside of school, I think we lived in a young boy's paradise. Saquoit had lots of snow in the winter, fairly early springs, hot summers, and falls with plenty of leaves and very mild trick or treating weather. We rented an old farmhouse and lived there all three years. My dad, who was the best handyman I have ever known (mechanic, electrician, plumber, carpenter, painter, you name it), could do it all. He cut a deal on the rent and was constantly fixing the place up for the owner of the house. I really hope he never did pay rent, because you couldn't even recognize the place when we left. The house sat on a couple of acres of property which included a one-stall garage, a shed, and a small barn. There were pear, apple, plum, and cherry trees and a large yard.

Our house in New York sat on a lazy country road between town and nowhere. Next door was a retired elderly couple and spread along our road were families with kids of similar ages to my sisters and me. The Schreks and Lemiouxs were the only families with high-school-aged kids. We had a small wooded area and cornfields behind us and fields and a turkey farm across the street. Behind the turkey farm was a creek that meandered through some trees and went under a bridge farther down our road. I don't know how much my sisters remember about living in Saquoit, but as I grow older I feel like my years there were some combination of *Huck Finn, Forest Gump,* and those boys in the movie *Stand By Me.*

The *Huck Finn* reference would be the adventure—building hidden forts in the nearby woods, sleeping out on summer nights, playing in the cornfield, and exploring up and down the creek and trout fishing. I always thought we were so far away from the house when we went on these adventures. Years later my mom burst my bubble when she told me she could always see us from the kitchen or living room window.

The "Indian Joe" to my friends and me was the guy who worked at the turkey farm. He drove an old, rust bucket of a pick-up truck and always tore up and down our road coming and going to work. The guy ran over my dog Sparky and two of my friends' dogs. At least one summer was spent on our revenge.

RANDOM THOUGHT NUMBER SIX

When it comes down to an argument over nature or nurture, I usually side with nurture. My dad had a lot of skills. He was a mechanic, electrician, carpenter, plumber, and painter. He could pick up just about any instrument and play by ear and was excellent with math. I know I'm of the same gene pool and he spent countless hours trying to teach me these skills, but very few, if any at all, have surfaced in me. For the most part it doesn't seem to have skipped a generation, either. My son has not shown any of these talents. My daughter is an outstanding pianist and has a beautiful singing voice, both skills she should thank her mother for.

Back to revenge! Thinking back on the turkey farmer running over my dog, it was partly my fault. My dog, Sparky, and I were walking alongside the road on our way to Lemioux's. Sparky wandered out into the road and was hit by the speeding turkey farmer, who never stopped. The reason I say it was partially my fault is because prior to that tragic event, I had hit Sparky in the head with a baseball bat, a "Nellie Fox" 29 to be exact. Some of you might remember the "Nellie Fox" bat; it was like a log. For those of you who don't, bats were once selected by the player's name on the bat and the size, not a model number. Anyway, while I was swinging the bat in the backyard, Sparky walked up behind me, and I accidentally hit him in the head. It knocked him out and I thought he was dead. Sparky recovered but never walked a straight line after that. Even though Sparky veered into the road walking to Lemioux's, I'm convinced the turkey farmer could have avoided hitting him. Two neighborhood dogs later, my friends and I decided to seek our revenge.

We started out simple—just rattled the cages and got the turkeys all fired up and ran away when the turkey guy or his dog came after us. Next, we upgraded to letting turkeys out of the barns. It was fun but not enough. The turkey farmer's dog would always chase us, and we managed to get away. At some point we realized his dog was basically blind. I really don't remember who thought it up, but we decided to focus on the dog. Simple concept—dog for a dog—but none of us were dog killers. We got the dog to chase us down one of the driveways between the turkey barns. The driveway had a short, stone wall at the end. We jumped up on the wall and the dog ran right into it. We laughed like crazy. "Stupid Men" are easily amused, so yes we repeated this act of revenge several times. And the dog always fell for it and ran into the wall. We were always greatly amused, and the dog never did figure it out. I don't know what the turkey farmer thought, but as far as my friends and I were concerned, revenge was ours!

RANDOM THOUGHT NUMBER SEVEN

If you ever want to be, or are, a leader of men, remember the "mouse in the corner" theory. Picture a small group of men trying to make a decision on what to do next. If you could be a mouse in the corner, you would witness who first proposed the idea and who was the first to say, "That's a great idea." If you can ever figure out who these two men are, you can get that group to do almost anything.

Every once in a while, my friends and I got to walk to town or up to school for baseball practice. Going to town was usually to cash in soda bottles for the refunds and buy candy with the profits. (Notice, I said "soda." I grew up saying "soda" until we moved to Minnesota in 1975, where I quickly learned the term "pop" to survive. I guess that was a random thought, but I'm sure it will be revisited.) The first time I saw the movie *Stand by Me,* the scenes where the boys hiked along the railroad tracks brought back memories of walking to town, because part of the walk was along a railroad track, but there was no bridge.

The challenge was on hot days or when time was of the essence. Along the way was a barbed wire fenced field with a few cows and a bull in it. The walk to town was shorter if you cut across the field.

Like any other "Stupid Man," I have always searched for shortcuts from here to there. The bull was very protective of the cows and would always chase us across the field. After a few close calls, we decided we needed a decoy. One quick game of mumbly peg or bloody knuckles would decide who would be the decoy. The loser would jump the fence and run the other way. As soon as the bull gave chase the rest of us would run across the field, jump the fence and wait for the decoy to rejoin us. Yeah, we lost time waiting, but for everyone except the decoy the walk to town was a shorter distance. Lesson learned and not put to use as an adult: every shortcut saves time or distance, but rarely do you get both.

The *Forest Gump* part of my life began in New York and to some degree has continued throughout my life. I'm referring to how Forest experienced history or was a part of history without really realizing it. This has probably happened to all of us, but here is my story.

RANDOM THOUGHT NUMBER EIGHT

On a recent trip, driving late at night (my favorite time to drive) on I-35 in southern Minnesota, I passed by a town that I hadn't been through in a while. I noticed a sign for an adult book and video store. I'm not positive, but I'm pretty sure the last time I was through this area, that same establishment was a BP gas station with a Happy Chef restaurant next to it. I know BP got hit with some serious financial losses over the oil spill in the Gulf of Mexico, but an adult bookstore? Also, if I had to choose, I'd take some sausage, pancakes, and eggs over porn every time, and I always liked standing in front of the Happy Chef statue and pushing the intercom button to see what he'd say.

Our family was visiting relatives in Philadelphia. My teenage cousin was a no-show for dinner. She showed up with her boyfriend well after dinner was over. I don't know why anyone would miss my Aunt Doris's spaghetti dinner. My cousin's boyfriend was, by all appearances, a bum—long hair, tattered clothes, grungy as all get out, and carried drumsticks. He sat in the living room and played an imaginary drum set. When I showed interest and curiosity, he ended up giving me the sticks, saying he carved his own anyway. Later, a major argument ensued between my aunt, uncle, and cousin. When it was done, my cousin and her boyfriend left.

Months later, my aunt, uncle, and cousin showed up at our house in New York. They stayed a couple of days and left my cousin to live with us and finish high school. I get it now—troubled teen, parents can't deal with her, move her out of the big city to upstate New York for some clean living and the guidance of her aunt and uncle. Three things happened while my cousin was there that all seemed weird at the time, but she explained to me years later. One day my cousin was babysitting my sisters and me. One of my friends came over and we took turns hitting golf balls in the yard. Somehow I got hit in the forehead by the golf club. I ran into the house bleeding profusely. I got to the bathroom and was rinsing the blood into the sink. My cousin absolutely freaked out but seemed very intrigued by the blood going down the drain. She explained later that she was tripping on LSD and couldn't believe my blood had so many different colors.

Second, there was a farm up on the hill near the school. In the summer, the farmer, who the high school kids called McDonald, would come around in the morning pulling a flatbed trailer behind a tractor. He would pick up anyone who wanted to come out to the farm and pick berries and be paid by the pint. He would also drop everyone off at the end of the day. The trailer was usually full, mostly with high school kids. What seemed odd at the time was you rarely saw any of the high school kids out in the fields. One day, I had to go to the barn to find farmer McDonald. As I approached the slightly open barn door, I couldn't help but notice a very odd smelling smoke billowing out of the doorway. I could hear loud music playing and upon entering the barn saw a bluish light spinning throughout the darkened barn. I'm also pretty sure I saw a few naked bodies. Later explanation: Farmer McDonald provided drugs to the teenage kids, and they partied all day while the younger kids, this "Stupid Man" included, picked berries. Explains why the high school kids, who usually slept on the way to the farm in the morning, were so much more interesting to watch and listen to on the way home at the end of the day.

And the third thing was my cousin at some point went missing—I don't know for how long, but I'm pretty sure a couple of days or more. My aunt even came up from Philadelphia. Eventually my cousin returned. Some years later she asked if I remembered that. I had but had no idea why she was gone; I just remembered my parents being in a panic. The explanation, the original "Woodstock," upstate New York, duh! Rest of the story: the boyfriend in Philadelphia was the drummer for the band Iron Butterfly.

The summer after fourth grade, my dad was transferred to Alameda Naval Air Station in Alameda, California. He was stationed on the U.S.S. *Hancock,* an aircraft carrier. I was jacked, to say the least. The Oakland Raiders had already been to the Super Bowl, and I had become a huge fan, especially of Daryl Lamonica, the "Mad Bomber." We also had relatives in the Los Angeles area that we had rarely seen. The only downside that I could see to this move was we'd be moving before the Little League season was over.

RANDOM THOUGHT NUMBER NINE

This is the best "Stupid Man" game my friends and I played in New York. We would stand in an open field in a circle. Someone would stand in the middle with the Hickory bow and an arrow. That guy would shoot the arrow straight up. We would watch the arrow until it disappeared from sight and watch for it to come back down and then scatter before it hit the ground. The one standing the closest to where the arrow stuck in the ground was the winner and got to shoot the next arrow. We spent several lazy afternoons playing that one. I don't even think the "mouse in the corner" could have figured out the genius behind that game.

In the summer of 1969, we moved to California. We made the trip down to Philadelphia to say goodbye to my relatives on my mom's side of the family. I don't think my dad was real popular at this time. I know my nana was not very excited to see her daughter and my sisters and me being taken out to California; there was that Charles Manson guy, all those hippies protesting the Vietnam War, and all those other lunatics living out there. No place to take a young family. Despite her protests, the trip out west continued.

We had done a lot of traveling together as a family, but never all the way to the West Coast. This was the classic trip in the Country Squire station wagon: my mom up front begging to stop to pee and the kids stretched out in the "way back." My dad was hardcore. We only stopped when we needed gas, and that is when we did everything as quickly as possible. Eat, go to the bathroom, change your clothes, and brush your teeth. All this had to be done while my dad put gas in the car, had some coffee, and stretched his legs. When he was ready to go that was it.

Superior, Wisconsin was our next destination point. I'm pretty sure my dad drove it straight through from Philadelphia to Superior. Most of my dad's side of the family was in the Duluth/Superior area or on the Iron Range in Minnesota, mostly in the Hibbing area. To this day, I do not know why Duluth/Superior is called the Twin Ports; they look nothing alike. We had a very enjoyable family reunion at a family cabin in Solon Springs, Wisconsin, and spent a day at Pool Location outside Hibbing, Minnesota. More goodbyes were said, and we were off to California.

My grandma came with us for this leg of the trip. She tried to change some of my dad's travel rules with minimal success. She tried desperately to get him to stop and see some of the sites along the way, but to no avail. To her credit, though, we did stop to stay at a motel in Salt Lake City, Utah. This was huge, because we never stayed in motels. We pulled into the motel in the dark and left prior to sunrise the next morning. I remember her lamenting about being in Salt Lake City and not getting to see the Great Salt Lake or the Mormon Tabernacle. My dad countered with, "You're not missing anything. It's like Lake Superior, only salty, and it's just another big church."

My grandma continued to protest. It just so happened that our motel was across the road from the lake. He walked her down to the water's edge, had her taste the water, and pointed out the tabernacle lit up on the horizon. "You've seen them both, now get in the car!" My dad was no millionaire, but once again, like the Beverly Hillbillies, we were off to California.

We lived in California for a little more than three years, for my fifth, sixth, seventh, and part of eighth grades. We moved there with a family of three kids, me and my two younger sisters, and left with four kids. My sister Stacie was born in 1971—twelve years younger than me. My guess is she was conceived between my dad's first and second deployments to Vietnam.

My Mom pretty much raised us kids on her own while we were in California. My dad had to do three long cruises to Vietnam during those years. California was great. We lived in Navy housing for the first and only time. The off-base housing was brand new. All the kids in the area were of similar ages to my sisters and me, and it seemed like everyone's dad was stationed on one of the aircraft carriers. The kids and the moms in the neighborhood were closely united I'm sure, by the common bond of having our dads/

husbands overseas most of the time. To this day I have a deeply rooted respect for my mother and any other military family wife/mother who has ever lived that lifestyle. It couldn't have been easy then, and it can't be now.

For the first time in my life I heard the term "Navy Brat." Kids from town and the civilians used it to identify us. I guess they thought we were spoiled. Thinking back on it, I would have a hard time arguing that we weren't. Aside from the fact our dads were gone most of the time, we had it pretty good. Living in Navy housing was great. We had gyms, pools, stores, tennis courts, and athletic fields at our disposal on the base. We had our own baseball, basketball, and flag football leagues. There were usually holiday parties for us when our dads were overseas, and I think my dad got a pretty good military family discount at Disneyland, Knott's Berry Farm, and Marine World.

I started fifth grade in a school on the base. I quickly developed my second teacher crush. Miss Stevens was gorgeous, and all the boys thought she looked like Barbara Eden, the *I Dream of Jeanie* version.

I don't know why, but for some reason some of us got moved to an elementary school in town. I don't know what the girls thought, but the boys were heartbroken. We even skipped school one day to go see Miss Stevens at our old school. The rest of fifth grade is pretty much a blur. I do remember taking Spanish for the first time, required in California, and I believe we had our first sex education class. Boys and girls had to go to separate rooms, and we weren't allowed to take the textbook out of the classroom. Pretty scary stuff, but no homework or outside reading.

RANDOM THOUGHT NUMBER TEN

Why is it that as I get older I like my wine redder and drier, my beer darker and heavier but my food lighter and less spicy?

My dad shipped out some time during our first fall in Alameda. The send-off for the carriers was very impressive. All the families were there to send off their loved ones. There were also protestors outside the base gates and some in small boats out in the San Francisco Bay. After the carrier left the dock, you were able to drive out on to the Golden Gate Bridge and wave goodbye, and the whole crew would be up on the main deck waving back. It was also fun to watch the carrier plow through the protesters' boats that were trying to prevent the carrier from leaving the bay. I may be a "Stupid Man," but even I know a bunch of fishing boats are not going to slow down an aircraft carrier. You do have to appreciate the passion and dedication of the protestors, though.

For the next nine months we communicated with my dad via letters and cassette tapes we would record and send back and forth. I do not recall any phone calls, and there was definitely no internet, texting, or emailing at that time. Any day we received correspondence from my dad was a great day. We would listen to the cassette tapes over and over until the next one arrived in response to what we would send him.

Sometime that fall I attended my first Oakland Raiders game. This was my first time in a professional stadium, the Alameda County Coliseum. I still get excited any time I step into a big stadium for the first time. The game was against the San Diego Chargers. I loved the Raiders, but it was fun to see Lance Alworth play, too. Mr. Harrison took me to the game. He was a youth recreation director on the base and coached most of the sports I played. Mr. Harrison lived a few houses away from us and was very influential in my life, with my dad being away. He served as my sponsor when I was confirmed. In the spring, Mr. Harrison brought me to a charity basketball game the Raiders were playing in and he was refereeing. After the game, he brought me into the locker room to meet the players. I still have a picture of Ben Davidson and me on my office wall.

Three concepts that Mr. Harrison instilled in me were 1) don't complicate things that can be kept simple; 2) delayed gratification; and 3) master one skill before moving on to another. These concepts were mostly learned through the way he coached me, especially when it came to pitching. He drilled it into me to throw the fastball for strikes and pitch for outs, not necessarily strikeouts. He always taught that every inning you went on the field your team needed three outs, any way you could get them. Eventually he started to teach me to throw change-ups, but was adamant about no curve balls. He worried about physical damage to my young arm, but mainly wanted me to have the confidence to rely on my fastball when I needed to throw a strike. The curveball would come later, when I was ready.

RANDOM THOUGHT NUMBER ELEVEN

Bull Durham is one of my favorite movies. Two of Mr. Harrison's teachings are in the movie: throwing the fastball for strikes and delayed gratification.

Experiencing Christmas in California was full of firsts. I received my first gas powered plane, which was my second favorite Christmas present, next to the electric football game I had received the year before. I had the one with the Packers and Raiders. It was a great toy and required serious strategizing, such as putting the linebacker that always spun around in the middle of your defense to screw up your opponent's offense and figuring out which one of your running backs was the fastest. I never was too good at passing or kicking those tiny, felt footballs. A lot of you reading this have no idea what I'm talking about, but I know there are other "Stupid Men" who get it. Luckily, I didn't get too attached to the plane because it crashed and burned on its third or fourth flight. Remote control was not part of the technology at the time.

It was also our first Christmas without snow and the first time I ever saw people decorate with paper bag luminaries in front of their houses. The no snow at Christmas was actually kind of depressing. I wouldn't mind experiencing the no snow for Christmas thing as an adult, just to see if I feel the same way.

The hardest part about our first holidays in California was not having my dad home on Christmas for the first time. Listening to him on cassette tapes or unwrapping presents from him and sending him our own family cassette tapes, cards, and presents just didn't make it any better. I'm sure it is a little better today for military families that can communicate with deployed loved ones via a computer, but there is nothing that compares to having a family all together on a holiday.

This was also the first Christmas I was hit with the cold, sad fact that there is no Santa Claus. Yeah, I was in fifth grade. I had suspected it, but up until this point had managed to suppress the thought. Another "Stupid Man" trait surfacing—suppress bad thoughts until you absolutely have to face them. I feel lucky I made it to the fifth grade believing in Santa Claus. Deep down, though, I'm still a believer. The fantasy ended on Christmas Eve, after my sisters went to bed, and my mom asked me to help take out the Christmas presents and put them under the tree. I tried to hide my shocked state and helped.

RANDOM THOUGHT NUMBER TWELVE

I don't remember how old my son Blaine was at the time, but I convinced my wife that Blaine would enjoy an electric football game from Santa Claus for Christmas. I tried to get him to play it several times but to no avail. He hated it! His object of desire was a GI Joe General Headquarters. A warning to other "Stupid Men": when you see advertising for retro toys such as Battling Tops, Rock'em Sock'em Robots, Battleship, Atari, etc. and think your son might like it, forget it! The marketing is designed to sucker us in. I find this to be very unfair. My daughter, Lexie, loved Barbies: the car, the dream house, all of it.

My dad returned home from Vietnam late in the spring. He had been gone for about nine months. I went to the big reception at the pier, and I got to go onto the aircraft carrier. Reuniting with my dad after this cruise and the next two times are three of my favorite childhood memories. The excitement and emotions in your family and the other families on the pier as they greet their fathers and husbands is overwhelming.

The first night he was back, my dad fulfilled a promise he had made when he left nine months previous. He promised to take me to an Oakland Athletics game when he got back. That night we went to see the A's play the Twins. We sat way up in the upper deck and froze in the cold, San Francisco Bay area wind. Several seats were open down below and the people sitting in those areas of the stadium appeared to be warmer. My dad is the most honest and honorable person I have ever known. He proved that over and over again during his time on earth, up until he died in 1989. On this night at the baseball game, he proved it twice. One, he took me to see the A's play his first night back in town. Second, he refused to move to seats in the lower parts of the stadium. He said, "You sit in the seats you pay for."

I look back on that night with the joy of knowing that I attended my first professional baseball game with my dad and it was his first also. I can't help but wonder if my dad was also somewhat of a "Stupid Man." He had been gone overseas for nine months, and I'm sure my mom had other plans for his first night back in town.

RANDOM THOUGHT NUMBER THIRTEEN

To women looking for "Mr. Right": He is the guy who will eat the burnt toast or stale cookies you and your children won't, and he doesn't consider being with his children to be babysitting. He will be home after work without stopping off at the bar first. Most likely he can't dance and doesn't have the best fashion sense. You can also count on him to buy you Christmas, anniversary, and birthday presents that he will have thought long and hard about, but you will want to return. Don't feel bad about that; he will either forget it or get over it and try again next year. Although he may not readily admit it, he knows you make him a better person and a little less "Stupid."

Most of the first summer in California was spent playing Little League baseball, going on camping trips for Boy Scouts, and going on a couple of family trips to Southern California to see my Aunt Margie—my dad's sister—and her family. We made our first visit to Disneyland, and I got to go to a California Angel game with my dad, uncle, and cousins. My cousins lived in a very "Brady"-like neighborhood in Orange Grove, conveniently located near Disneyland, Knott's Berry Farm, Anaheim Stadium, and only a short drive to the beach.

It was nice to have my dad home. He went on some of the camping trips for Boy Scouts, attended my baseball games, and even umpired a couple of them. I recall being called out by him on the bases and wouldn't talk to him for a couple of days. To this day, I swear I was safe. As honest as he was, though, I was probably out. What "Stupid Man" would tell a baseball story where he was out? We all know that with age the homeruns get longer and our velocity increases and our batting averages go up every time we tell the story. However, despite my dad's reputation, I'm sticking with that I was safe!

Our Boy Scout troop on the base was very well funded. In the three years we were in California, I had the experience of camping at Big Sur, the Sierra-Nevada Mountains, Sonora, Pico Blanco, some beach north of San Francisco, and Presidio. We also took a bike trip through San Francisco and across the Golden Gate Bridge to Sausalito, and we toured Alcatraz Island. The highlight trips were our three 100+ mile excursions. They were all week-long trips in three consecutive summers. The first two were 100 mile hikes through remote parts of Yosemite National Park. The third was a 100 mile canoe trip on the American River. We had to train and do qualifying trips for all three, so it was an honor to be chosen to go. I was also lucky enough to obtain Eagle Scout and be chosen for the Order of the Arrow while participating in Boy Scouts.

I don't remember much about the sixth grade except for a very strict and demanding teacher, Mr. Bosworth. He was the first teacher that mentioned on my report card that I seemed distracted and not real focused on my schoolwork during baseball season. I do recall having a similar problem in college when I was playing baseball. After my college graduation, my mom asked why I didn't graduate with honors. I told her I wouldn't have been able to sit with my "Stupid" friends at the graduation ceremony.

In sixth grade I learned a little street survival. A city park and Chipman Junior High School were between my elementary school and home. If you got caught in the park by the junior high kids before or after school you usually got beat up or harassed. The group of friends that I walked with became very skilled at avoiding these kids. It was a daily event to change routes and timing. We ran across car ports, cut through buildings, hid in stores, and hopped fences and walls. When we were feeling cocky, we sprinted across the park. We got caught occasionally but for the most part survived the daily round trip.

Any time an aircraft carrier left the base, student protestors from UC-Berkley would show up. When this happened, all the kids in the military housing assembled at a corner and we would either be bussed or escorted by military police to school. There would be jeeps in front of and behind us and helicopters overhead—not exactly a covert operation. On these days, we had to come to school early to sit in the cafeteria and wait for a school-wide attendance to be taken. Usually after hearing our names read off, some of my friends and I would sneak out to go watch the protestors and throw a few rocks at them before running back to school. I'm not sure why we did this. I do remember being very upset and confused and wondering why these people were protesting something I was so proud of my dad for doing. I was proud that my dad was in the Navy and fighting in the Vietnam War and confused as to why these protestors thought that was wrong.

Sixth grade was the last year we had recess. Four square, handball, and basketball were my favorite playground games. Football was fun also, but tackle football on the blacktop was tough on school clothes. Remember when our clothes were categorized? School clothes, work clothes, play clothes, church clothes, etc. My dad took this to a whole different level. I'm pretty sure he had one dress suit; the proof is in pictures. He always wore the same suit for weddings, funerals, first communions, confirmations, and graduations.

Anyway, the end of recess was noted by a bell. When the bell went off, everyone on the playground had to stand perfectly still. When one of the playground monitors tapped you on the shoulder, you could go back to class. I'm sure this was to avoid a chaotic rush back into the school building. Sometime during my sixth grade year, and this could just be an urban legend but I remember it as real, there was a serial killer in the Bay Area. He was called Scorpio or something to do with a zodiac sign. He was locating himself on rooftops and shooting kids. If he was ever by our school and sitting on a rooftop with a rifle watching our playground, he must have decided it was too easy and cut us a break.

My sister Stacie was also born in January of my sixth grade year, which completed our family of me and three younger sisters. My dad flew home for a few days when she was born. The rest of us kids thought it was to see Stacie. Apparently, that was not military protocol. The truth was my mom had had severe complications and almost died giving birth. As soon as it was determined that she was going to be okay, he was flown back to rejoin the aircraft carrier in Vietnam. I reveled in having a new baby sister. I did not know that this would be the sister that would rebel against my authority as the older brother. Terri and Lisa always followed my lead and would do almost anything I asked of them. As Stacie grew older, this was not true of her.

The summer after sixth grade was all about baseball. I made the all-star team that got to travel all over the place. We won several tournaments, including the All-Forces tournament for the state of California. On several days, members of the Oakland A's would coach us at practices and games when they could. Some of them were in the Naval Reserves, and this is how they logged their hours. I specifically remember Rick Monday, Joe Rudi, Reggie Jackson, and Vida Blue being at practices or games. On Little League Day at an A's game, all the teams in the Oakland-Alameda area sat in the upper deck, but our team sat in box seats by the A's dugout. One day at practice one of the players brought us new uniforms and hats. The pants were white and the jerseys were green with white and gold trim and had "Athletics" tackle twilled across the chest. The hats were replicas of the Oakland A's hats. We were called the

Alameda Athletics after that. The uniform was the first non-wool uniform I ever played in. It was some new material, and I'm guessing it was polyester.

We continued to win tournaments and were going to the region tournament. For some reason, by the Little League powers that be, we were removed from the tournament and deemed ineligible. I grew up thinking it was because we were all technically from different hometowns. Years later I had the opportunity to meet Tommy John at a baseball tournament in Brainerd, Minnesota. In our conversation he found out I was one of the kids on that team. He said that when he and Rick Monday played together with the Dodgers. Rick would tell stories about us all the time. He described us as a bunch of freaks. We were pretty good as I recall. We did go undefeated—a very talented bunch of 12-year olds. Because of our size, we had to have birth certificates with us as proof of age everywhere we played. Tommy told me that Rick said the reason we were deemed ineligible for advancement to the Little League World Series was because the Little League Association accused the Navy of assembling us on one Naval Base. Seriously, the Navy found us all over the country when we were 10, put our dads on aircraft carriers and sent them to Vietnam so their sons could play baseball and represent Alameda Naval Air Station in the Little League World Series? I know the government was doing some odd things in the late '60s and early '70s, but come on. Thinking back, I do remember that the last team we played we beat by more than 10 runs. They were reinstated into the regionals and went on to the World Series. It is also true that I was the only 10-year-old on the Saquoit, New York travel team the last summer we lived in New York. Conspiracy or not?

RANDOM THOUGHT NUMBER FOURTEEN

Today is day number 14 of the Minnesota State Government shutdown. Our governor and congressional leaders can't agree on a budget. The Republicans are blaming the Democrats and vice versa. People are finally getting mad. There was a union protest in Duluth and a Senior Citizens' protest at the capitol building in St. Paul. I haven't heard anything yet today, but I'm sure a compromise will come quickly now. First, people were a little upset because you couldn't buy a fishing license and the state lottery was closed. Now it has gone too far! The Minneapolis Star

Tribune ran an article on bars and liquor stores closing in Minneapolis because they can't renew their liquor licenses. The crap really hit the fan last night on the 10:00 news. It was announced that Coors and Miller Beer will not be distributed in Minnesota because their distributing license has run out. People were somewhat upset when state workers were laid off, rest areas were closed, and several state-funded programs were cut-off. Wait and see the uproar when Minnesotans can't fish, drink, or gamble. Our summers are only two months long the way it is, and now this! Throughout this shutdown, I can't help but wonder if our government would be more efficient without political parties. It is not about checks and balances or watchdogs anymore. It seems to be more about leaders afraid to make tough decisions and parties more concerned with setting the other party up to fail, instead of just coming together and agreeing on prudent fiscal, legal, and moral plans for governing our states and country. My wife does a great job of maintaining our household budget. She also does an outstanding job of running her own business, the Mitchell-Tappan House Bed & Breakfast. I am her only employee and despite being unpaid, I have to say she treats me well. She does a good job with marketing and public relations. She promotes Hibbing, Minnesota and the surrounding area. We entertain several foreign guests every year and she handles them very well. Could it possibly be that we have too many "Stupid Men" running our government? As my players might say, "Just saying."

Seventh grade was highlighted by the move to Chipman Junior High School, which fed into Encinal High School. The first thought was that we'd no longer have to run home to avoid being beat up by the junior high kids in the park. Once we got past first day initiation from eighth graders it would be smooth sailing. Wrong! The ninth graders from the high school were the new nemesis in the park. I guess since they were at the bottom of the pecking order at the high school, they needed someone to pick on.

Other than not having recess, junior high was pretty neat. We got to choose a class schedule, had multiple teachers, and were given lockers. I also began to notice that we had girls in school with us, and some of them were pretty good looking and smelled good. We had dances and talent shows. The dances were usually held after school in the gym. It was the same gym that we had our basketball games and P.E. classes in, but turn off some lights, throw in some decorations and black lights, and you've hit the big time. My first slow dance was with Jenny Paige, and the song was "Just My Imagination" by the Temptations. As far as talent shows go, I've already told you I had none. My friend Mark and I did enter once, though. We did a lip sync duo. My friend Mark, who was black, did Donny Osmond and I did Michael Jackson. I'm white, which did make a difference when Michael was younger. We did two songs: "One Bad Apple" and "ABC's." We finished second to an eighth grade band that did "The House of the Rising Sun." I don't remember what the winners got, but we won free Slurpees and a taco from the local Seven Eleven.

Despite these newfound distractions at school, sports remained my passion. We had intramural leagues that led into the try-outs for school teams. I played football, basketball, and baseball. Intramurals were fun, but it was really exciting to play for a school team. We were the Chipman Cougars. There were several other junior high schools on the island and in Oakland that we played against. At home games, we even had cheerleaders; Jenny Paige was a cheerleader. We got to organize our own intramural teams and Mr. Fox and Mr. Grant, our P.E. teachers, set up a noontime schedule. They also coached the school teams, so if they liked what they saw, you were invited to play for the school. I usually captained an intramural team, so I was always scouting out the talent around school and recruiting before any season started.

Bill Russell's son was in my P.E. class. I had never seen him play basketball, but I figured if Bill Russell was his dad, he had to be a player, so I asked him to be on my team. He was terrible! As a college coach today, I try not to get too excited about the bloodlines of prospective recruits until I've seen them play. I may be a "Stupid Man," but I like to think I'm not a stupid coach.

Mr. Fox and Mr. Grant were very tied into the professional and college sports community in the Bay Area. Mr. Fox was a young guy who had played as a lineman at Stanford and had a try-out with the 49ers. Mr. Grant was older and had played briefly in the AFL. I remember both had bad knees. Occasionally players from the Raiders, 49ers, San Francisco Warriors, and Stanford would stop by and talk to us at P.E. classes or practices. I actually got to meet Fred Biletnikoff. He laughed when one of my teammates asked him about using stick' em to help catch a football. I was a quarterback, so the day that Jim Plunkett stopped by was huge. He signed my practice jersey before practice, but it got sweated out that day. I idolized Mr. Fox and Mr. Grant. Being a P.E. teacher and coach seemed very appealing. It would be a good back-up plan to playing a professional sport.

RANDOM THOUGHT NUMBER FIFTEEN

Beginning with my dad, there have been many older adult males in my life that have had a positive, life- impacting influence on me: my uncles, Gene, Mike, Joe, Lynn, and John; coaches, Mr. Harrison, Mr. Fox, Mr. Grant, George Marsnik, Bob Montebello, and Bob Altuvilla; and mentors, Rod Loe, Lowell Roisum, Jim Sundstrom, Dennis Kaatz, Terry Teiken, Bud Ode, Blacky Variano, Rudy Marolt, Steve Kerzie, Art Westphal, Dan Bergan, Rick Tintor, Al Holmes, Pastor Jack Harris, and Bill Wirtanen, just to name a few. These men have all come in and out of my life in various stages of growing up as a kid or in my professional career. Only some of them are still in my life today, but all of them are still in my heart and very much a part of who I am.

I've been thinking about what they all possibly have in common. They are all passionate people, dedicated to their families, and whether they know it or not, had and have a huge impact on me and I'm sure scores of other younger men and women. They are all leaders in their own right and are men of their word. None of them are perfect, but all worthy role models. I just want to take a second to thank them for being a part of my life. We need more people like this in this world. In my lifetime, there have been plenty of men in the public eye and positions of authority that have abused that authority with questionable acts, promises, and claims. Richard Nixon: "I am not a crook.!" Bill Clinton: "I did not have sex with that woman!" Barry Bonds: "I did not take performance enhancers!" Tiger Woods: "We're all addicted to something!" Charlie Sheen: "Duh, winning!" And even more recently, Anthony Weiner: "My computer got hacked." I could go on, but I digress. You get my point. I hope I can live up to the legacy passed on to me by the men originally listed and have a life-long positive influence on my children, their children, and the young men and women I coach and teach. One thing that worries me, though, is that I know several of these men that I owe my gratitude to have been accused of being "Stupid Men" by loved ones, players, students, fans, etc. That said, if this is some kind of a club or fraternity, I want in.

My dad returned home from his third cruise to Vietnam sometime late that year. The U.S.S *Hancock* was dry docked in San Diego this time, so he had to go there. I think it had been dry docked in San Francisco after the first two cruises. We had been in California for three years, and it was now time to move again. Eventually, my dad received his orders; we were moving to New Jersey. He would be stationed at Lakehurst Naval Air Station. He was going to be some kind of instructor at a training school on the base. I know my dad was a chief petty officer and did some kind of electrical work. He was going to teach something about a gyro that was used for navigation on ships.

We weren't moving right away, so I started my eighth grade year at Chipman Junior High, and we moved sometime that fall. It was tough moving again after three years but exciting at the same time. My sisters, Terri and Lisa, and I knew the drill. Stacie was clueless, but she wasn't even two yet, so it didn't matter.

Before closing my thoughts on our time in California, I would be remiss if I didn't mention Billy Moody. Billy was my best friend almost the whole time we lived in California. We have not spoken since my family moved. I think my mom has had some contact with the Moodys over the years. Billy and I did most everything together other than play baseball. I hope he still has some of the memories I have of those times. I do know the two of us together usually meant some kind of trouble for us and our mothers. Couple of quick stories—yeah, right; anyone that has ever known me knows I can't tell a quick story.

In fifth grade we took a class trip to San Quentin Penitentiary. We toured the yard, walked the wall, and then got to go into a cell block. After going through a series of doors and gates, we were standing at one end of a female cell block. The inmates left the other end of the cell block to go to lunch. We lined up in pairs in front of the cells, and Billy and I were together. We were told that when the cells were opened we could go in and look around for a couple of minutes and were not to touch anything. When done we would all leave the cell block together. While looking around, one of us noticed *Playboy* magazines under the bed. What "Stupid Man" can think straight in the presence of naked women, even if just in pictures—forget the articles. We were supposed to be leaving the cell block soon. Somehow we didn't notice our class had left the cell block and all was quiet. Problem was the cells closed and we were locked in. We yelled for the class, our teacher, the guards, anyone, but apparently nobody heard us. Minutes later a red light flashed and a bell went off at the end of the cell block where we had entered. It was the female prisoners back from lunch. They marched in and stood in pairs in front of their cells and yelled back to the guards as role was called out. We had two large women standing in front of us, threatening to do God knows what to us when that cell door opened. Both Billy and I screamed and cried for help. Luckily one of the guards heard us. The guard came to the cell and saved what we were sure was our lives. The prisoners were all removed from the cell block, and we were escorted out and brought back to the tour group. Billy and I had to visit with our teacher, the principal, and a psychologist after school for the next couple of weeks. I think they were checking to see if we had been emotionally scarred. The only question we had was why were there *Playboy* magazines in a female jail cell? Nobody seemed to want to explain that to us, and I don't remember covering it in our sex education class. I put it in the anonymous question box in class, but the teacher never addressed it.

At some point we convinced our mothers to let us ride the city bus, just a quick trip to our favorite candy store and back. This store, unlike the exchange on the base, had Suzy Q's, baseball cards with the large piece of gum and those large Sweet Tarts. We convinced our moms we could do it. We got to the store okay, but on the return trip home ended up on the wrong bus and made our way across the Bay Bridge to San Francisco. A lot of crying and pleading later and by the grace of one very sympathetic bus driver we were brought back to Alameda and returned to the custody of our mothers. I really don't remember if we were punished, but I still remember the trip to San Francisco.

One last Billy Moody story: One of our mothers dropped us off at the movie theater on the base to meet some other friends and see *The Incredible Mr. Limpet*. I'm not sure if that was the name of it, but I think it starred Don Knotts and he was an animated fish who went under the sea and helped the U.S. Navy sink German subs in World War ll. On this particular night, though, we waited and none of our friends showed up. The line kept getting longer, and it was all sailors. We stayed in line and when we got to the ticket booth we were questioned about our age. A couple of sailors behind us told the girl selling tickets that we were with them. We got in, got our popcorn and sat down. The theater was packed—two twelve-year-old boys and a bunch of rowdy sailors. The cartoons came on and then the feature show. Not *Mr. Limpet* and not rated "G." I believe it was rated "X." I'm not sure what that got you in 1970, but every time I uncovered my eyes there was skin. After the movie was over, we exited to find both our moms out front. Again, I don't remember the punishment, but we saw skin.

Billy, if you are still out there, thanks for those memories and all the others: camping trips, sidewalk roller derby, pick-up football, smear the queer (slaughter, kamikaze, or whatever name you called it—the game where everyone tackled the guy with the football), all of it. I don't know about you, but I haven't been back to prison, ridden on a city bus, or been to an "X' rated movie since then. Hope all is well with you. Don't bother looking for me on Facebook—I'm not on it.

Heading back to the East Coast, my mom was going home again, close to Philadelphia and her side of the family. We didn't know it at the time, but this would be my dad's last station in the Navy. I suspect my parents knew, but my sisters and I did not.

I was excited because we had never lived in New Jersey but had been to the shore several times. I also knew it meant Hoagies, Cheese Steaks, Italian Ices, and Tastykakes, and also the Phillies, Eagles, Sixers, and Flyers. I would also get to see my cousin Eugene again. He was one of three cousins my age. His twin sister, Joanne, and my cousin, Joe, were the other two. Eugene and I were pretty close, though, and I missed him when we were in California.

We made the move to New Jersey in the fall of 1972. We stayed in a motel for a little while, though I don't know whether we were waiting for our stuff to arrive from California or my parents were looking for a place to live. We ended up moving into a house outside of Browns Mills, in a development called Country Lakes Estates. I think we lived there about a year before my parents bought a house in Browns Mills. Even if you are not from New Jersey, you might recognize the name Browns Mills. It was where the aliens landed in the original radio broadcast of the War of the Worlds. I also remember hearing once that he *Philadelphia Enquirer* ran a promotion in which they gave away free plots of land in Browns Mills if you bought a subscription. The catch was the plots weren't big enough to build on.

My sisters and I were enrolled at schools in the Pemberton Township School District. I attended one of several junior highs that fed into Pemberton High School and picked up with eighth grade again. Pretty much the same as Chipman, but I couldn't take Spanish anymore so I replaced it with French. It was also odd to be back in a school where everything was enclosed. The classrooms in the schools in California all opened to the outside. It was very crowded in the hallways at my new school. I must have mentioned this observation to one of my teachers because I was chosen to be a hall monitor shortly after enrolling at the school.

It was great to be the new kid at school again. I have always found it interesting to meet new people and experience different ways of doing things. We moved to New Jersey too late to play football, but I was able to make the basketball and baseball teams. I really only have vivid memories of two of my teachers. Mr. Fisher was an elderly gentleman who taught physical education. He always claimed he invented the game "Crab Soccer." I don't know if he did, but I do know it seemed liked we played it just about every day we couldn't go outside. I don't remember the name of my English teacher, but I know I did very well in her class. It was because of her and my Uncle Gene, who was an English teacher and football coach at Eddystone H.S. and later Ridley Park outside of Philadelphia, that I flirted with the idea of pursuing a career related to English and writing. Sometime during the year I qualified with a few other students to go with our English teacher to see Rod McKuen at the Philadelphia Philharmonic. Dinner and a show—pretty exciting stuff. Our teacher was pretty excited about it, and so were we. We had to spend two weeks boning up on our Rod McKuen—not my favorite poet, but it was still worth it to make the trip into Philadelphia.

Finally the big day arrived, and our teacher and a few students loaded into a school van and drove over to Philadelphia. We ate in some fancy downtown restaurant, for which all of us students had to learn proper dining etiquette. After dinner we made our way over to the Philharmonic. When we got there and saw the billboard, it was George Carlin that was performing that night, not Rod McKuen. Our teacher went in to double check. I don't know if our teacher was excited about the change, but I know we were. We took a vote and unanimously decided to watch George Carlin. The permission slips our parents had signed were to watch Rod McKuen, so this was a bold move our teacher was making. I have never seen McKuen perform, but I enjoyed the George Carlin performance immensely. He did a concert in which he started out as a baby in the womb and finished as a senile old man. Great show! It was funny, sad, and very entertaining. To this day, despite how well plans may be laid, I am always open to a change of schedule. You just never know how something might turn out.

The rest of eighth grade just flew by, pretty much a blur. December was tough; I got my heart broken. The Steelers defeated my beloved Raiders via the "Immaculate Reception." A lot of people in New Jersey were excited because Franco Harris was a Jersey boy and played his football at Rancocas Valley. I also started my career in the newspaper industry. I took a paper route in our neighborhood delivering the *Trenton Times*. I did the route on my bike. Loved delivering but hated it when it was time to collect from my customers. People would try everything to make it hard to collect: lock their yard gates, leave their ill-tempered dogs out in the yard, or put up notes that they were out of town. Besides babysitting my sisters, this was my first paid job. Seemed like a lot of work for minimal pay, but it was a job and I kept it until we moved to our new house in Browns Mills.

Summer that year was great. I played Babe Ruth baseball, made several trips over to Philadelphia, and got to go to the New Jersey shore anytime the opportunity presented itself. We also made the move to our new house in Browns Mills. This was also about the time I got another dog. He was a mutt—black, silver, and white—Oakland Raider colors—so I named him "Raider." He was a great companion but had a mind of his own. Like most other dogs I've had in my life, he loved to run off anytime he got the chance and also loved to chew up the grass in the backyard.

That summer I also learned I was an expendable part of our family. I don't know if this was because I was the oldest child or because it was my dog who kept chewing up the grass in the backyard. I got braces that summer and my orthodontist was in Tom's River, New Jersey. My mom would drive to Tom's River on the New Jersey Turnpike to bring me to my appointments. Quite often there would be loaded sod trucks on the Turnpike. On occasion rolls of sod would fall off the trucks. Without regard for traffic, my mom would stop the station wagon and tell me to get out and throw the sod roll in the back. It didn't matter what side of the road the sod was on; it was my newfound task to get out, dodge traffic, and retrieve the sod rolls. We did this often enough to sod a large part of our backyard. I guarded the new sod with my life and did all I could to keep Raider from chewing it up and putting me back on the Turnpike to retrieve more. I always have felt a close bond with my mom, but it went to a whole new level that summer, being partners in crime.

RANDOM THOUGHT NUMBER SIXTEEN

When I do something good or right around the house and my wife discovers it, she says, "You didn't do this, did you?" If I have done something wrong, she will say, "You did this, didn't you!" I have learned to admit to being a "Stupid Man," but I have become very aware of a seemingly acquired skill that many of the females in my life have mastered. I call it the question/statement or statement/question. Example: My wife and I are dressed to go out for dinner. She sees me and says, "You are not going to wear that, are you?"

In the written form, that phrase is followed by a question mark. When you hear the same phrase spoken, there is no question mark, and it is replaced by an exclamation point. Another example would be – and I hear this one more often from my wife as I get older – "Are you going to trim your eyebrows?" But the statement I have come to fear because it leaves me in an absolute state of confusion is, "I don't care, do what you want!" or "Just do what you think is right!" I don't know about the rest of the "Stupid Men" out there, but when I hear either one of these statements from my wife, I am frozen and cannot make a decision. This can only be a trap!

Summer came to an end, and a new phase was about to begin. Junior high was now a thing of the past, and high school was about to start. Ninth grade through twelfth grade students all attended Pemberton Township High School. I was now a freshman and would have to coexist with sophomores, juniors, and seniors. We were no longer identified by grade. From the first day of school on, it was evident that freshmen were the low end of the pecking order and survival skills needed to be learned quickly. I could only hope that some of the street skills I picked up in California would pay off.

We entered the first day of school with a little over 1,000 kids in our freshmen class. Pemberton High School was one of New Jersey's largest schools at the time—big enough that we had a split day schedule. Freshmen and sophomores attended in the afternoon and juniors and seniors attended in the morning. If a sophomore was on an athletic team, they went to school with the juniors and seniors. The first day of school was all about freshmen initiation. Forget about orientation, finding your classes, seeing if you could open your locker, and getting signed up for football tryouts—it was all about surviving the day without getting beaten up. Lucky for the freshmen, the juniors and seniors didn't have very long to have at us, as they had to go home or get to practice.

Freshmen initiation usually consisted of getting roughed up or your standard snuggies, swirlies, or de-pantsings. Several buses dropped us off at the doors. There were a couple thousand kids being dropped off for school and all the upperclassmen were waiting to take buses home. Somehow the upperclassmen were able to figure out who the freshmen were, and the terror began. I survived the first wave. As I was being chased down the hall, a kid grabbed me and asked if I had caught any freshmen yet. Even as a "Stupid Man," I could see this as a major reprieve. I said I had not and joined the chase to catch freshmen. I helped seek out kids from other junior highs than my own. Eventually, I was ratted out and received my just dues. After a couple of days, the initiations stopped and things settled in.

Ninth grade was great—school in the morning, practices and games in the afternoon, and back home again on the late bus. The only stress in my life was wearing that stupid face bow with my braces. You had to wear it so many hours per day. I wouldn't be caught dead wearing it at school, so it went on after dinner and stayed on until morning, most days. I'm pretty sure the orthodontic technology has advanced enough that kids don't have to go through that ordeal anymore. They should be thankful. I don't care who you were or how many kids you knew who wore the face bows, there was no way to look like anything but a nerd when you put it in and strapped it around your head. Sleeping and not drooling all over your pillow was impossible also.

I resumed my newspaper career that year also. This time the work was minimal, the pay and the benefits were great, and there was no collecting. My friend's dad was a newspaper vendor. He would take a small group of us over to Fort Dix and drop us off with a bundle of papers by the barracks and mess halls. We got paid per paper sold, and a little more on Sundays. The pay could be good, depending where you got dropped off. I learned a lesson in seniority, which was the longer you worked the better your drop off spot would be. As I said before, the benefits were great. The soldiers in basic training paid big money for candy, magazines, and cigarettes—a high profit margin if you knew what you were doing. The guys that did not have phone privileges would also give us money and a phone number to call. Usually we called mothers or girlfriends to pass on whatever message had been given to us. The soldier would give us an extra tip when we returned the message from home. If you spent enough days around the same barracks or mess halls, you got to know some of these guys pretty well, and the trust factor turned into specific food requests and higher profits. I actually got $10 once for a $2 Hoagie.

RANDOM THOUGHT NUMBER SEVENTEEN

I went to see the Tall Ships in Duluth, Minnesota a couple of weeks ago at the Maritime Music Festival. They have sailed to Duluth a few times, but this was my first time to see them. The ships were amazing to look at, and it was a beautiful day, about 92 degrees at Canal Park. Some of the ships sailed in the War of 1812, and that was probably the last time it was 92 degrees in Duluth. Duluth's weather notwithstanding, put viewing the Tall Ships on your bucket list. Every "Stupid Man" should develop an appreciation for history and quality craftsmanship. The musical entertainment was good, also.

I was in ninth grade in 1973-74. Two things happened on the national sports scene that year that I remember well. John Cappeletti won the Heisman Trophy playing for Penn State. John was from Upper Darby, Pennsylvania, which we lived near when I was younger. I was a huge Penn State fan then and today. Joe Paterno is one of the coaches I have always admired. It was also the year the Philadelphia Flyers won their first Stanley Cup. Even our high school took the day off for the celebration parade. There was also a gas shortage that year. Gas was rationed at the pumps. If your license plate ended in an odd number you could only get gas on odd days of the month and vice versa. Lines were long at the gas stations. Once again my mom proved I was expendable. She would let me sit at the wheel, and she would go grocery shopping. I would move the car forward in line as needed until she returned. Not as dangerous as picking up sod on the turnpike, but a criminal act nonetheless. The legal driving age in New Jersey was 17 at the time.

Besides all the normal high school stuff, my two years at Pemberton H.S. proved valuable to my social development. It was the only time in my life I can truly say I experienced being a minority. The student population was primarily black, and there was also a large Puerto Rican population. White was the minority, especially on athletic teams. We did have an occasional racial riot at school, and more often than not it was the Black and Korean students. Whenever a riot was threatened or took place, we got the day off. I think the administration called it a "Cooling Off Period." Being white and a member of an athletic team, especially the basketball team, had its perks. It didn't matter much as a freshman, but I would learn as a sophomore the benefits were huge. I never had much of a problem making friends and race has never been an issue with me, so blending in at school was not a problem as long as I didn't have to wear that face bow to school. Two of my closest friends were George, a black kid, and Felix, a Puerto Rican. The kid I admired the most at school was Eddie Meyers. I had the pleasure of playing one year of football with Eddie. He was by far the best athlete in our class and possibly the whole school. He later went on to be a running back at the Naval Academy and was one of the top backs in the country his junior and senior years. He was a man child in ninth grade and the rest of us just tried to exist in his world. He was probably the best athlete I ever had the experience of playing with or against. He dominated any sport he participated in.

Summer after ninth grade was great. I don't know if it had something to do with being post-puberty or what, but things just seemed to be a lot more exciting. Maybe it was because the first year of high school had been completed and our freshman year was over and we had all survived it. All I know is it all felt different. I felt a little more adult-like in some way. I felt a confidence I hadn't ever felt. I was always a confident; some might say cocky, kid. I'll say self assured, but this was different. Okay, two things that would explain this would be post-puberty and I got my braces off—no more face bow. Now it was time to get serious.

RANDOM THOUGHT NUMBER EIGHTEEN

I live in Hibbing, Minnesota. We have cable television in our home. My favorite sports channel after ESPN is the Big Ten Network, which our cable network does not provide. Our cable company provides three shopping networks, four news networks, four PBS stations, HGTV, Food Channel, Oxygen, WE, and the Speed Channel. We now have MC 22, which covers Iowa sports from Little League up to the Iowa Barnstormers, an arena football team. I would trade every one of them to have the Big Ten Network.

The summer started out like every summer since I was six, with baseball tryouts. My Babe Ruth team was a good one. We went on to win the league title, and I was chosen to play on a 15-year-old all-star team, which traveled late into the summer. We got as far as the Mid-Atlantic play-offs.

That summer was also a time to increase my income. I continued to sell newspapers on the Fort Dix Army Base, and I also took a job picking commercial blueberries on a farm not too far from home. I made pretty good money picking blueberries, but what made the job great was lunchtime. My mom always packed a good lunch, but that wasn't the highlight. The highlight was the girls that were working there. Every once in a while we'd sneak off to the lake and go swimming and some underwater playful groping eventually turned into some making out with the girls who weren't completely offended by the groping. Definitely not the most politically correct relationship with fellow employees, but definitely reason to show up at work every day.

For some reason this is also the summer that I staged somewhat of a mini rebellion against my parents. I somehow talked them into leaving me behind when my sisters, mom, and dad went to Niagara Falls. We were in a big baseball tournament, and I just wasn't going to miss it. I have since made it to Niagara Falls on my own twice. The baseball tournament was in the Atlantic City area. We were eliminated from the tournament early, so we had time to kill. A couple of our coaches were college-aged kids. They suggested going to the boardwalk to hopefully catch some of the free concert. We got there before the concert started, so we hit the beach and walked the boardwalk for a while. The coaches taught us a new game. Definitely a game for "Stupid Men," but training at the same time.

Somebody would pick a random person off the beach or boardwalk and declare a category that they thought matched the person. Examples of categories were, girl, boy, married, single, over 18, under 18, gay, transvestite, etc. The person who had picked put a dollar down. If you disagreed, you put a dollar down and declared what you thought the person was. The guy that had made the original pick had to ask the person. If you were right you got the money and had the next pick. This game proved to be just as dangerous as the bow and arrow game. A wrong judgment of character often resulted in a slap or some harsh words. I still can't help thinking that this game helped in some way later in life when it was critical to have to make snap judgments about people. I consider myself a pretty good judge of character, but I have learned that first impressions are rarely correct if you get the time to actually know a person.

The free concert was one I'll never forget. It was a dream come true for any Jersey Boy in the 1970s; live on the Atlantic City Boardwalk were Southside Johnny and the Asbury Jukes and Bruce Springsteen! The story our coaches had us tell at home was that we had been at the baseball tournament, lost in the semi-final, and stuck around to watch the championship.

I only attended four concerts while in high school. The second one was later that summer. I don't know what lie I told to get to that one; you make that stuff up in the heat of the moment and shouldn't be held accountable thirty-seven years later. The concert was at Veterans Stadium in Philadelphia. It was a classic '70s concert featuring, in no particular order, Yes, Mott the Hoople, Steve Miller Band, and Peter Frampton. Seeing any one of them would have been worth whatever it took, but to see all of them at one concert was definitely worth whatever it took to get there or any grounding I received afterward.

Summer ended with baseball at the top of my priorities. That and trying to get a date with Yvette Rios and trying to sneak a beer at a neighborhood barbecue. Baseball ended with a loss in the Mid-Atlantic regional, and playing so late in the summer caused me to miss the beginning of football practice, which made me ineligible. I did get to date Yvette, and my friends and I managed to sneak a can or two of beer.

RANDOM THOUGHT NUMBER NINETEEN

I do not text, nor do I have a Twitter or Facebook account. I do believe in social networking, though. I find some of my favorite places to do this are church, the local grocery store, the barbershop, our back patio, our front porch, coaches' meetings, the mailroom, faculty meetings, my office, volleyball and basketball practices and games, and wine club. I also enjoy the occasional pontoon ride with friends (Fall Lake Flotilla) and 4th of July in the park in Ely, Minnesota. Making a phone call or writing a letter every once in a while is also a healthy practice. I have become a user of email as of late, and I mean late, but it is pretty much business only. I have never updated my status, and I'm doing just fine.

Overall, I would call the summer of 1974 a banner summer

in my life. The most noteworthy accomplishment of the summer has to be credited to my sister Terri. As an athlete and a coach, I have always been a big believer in the importance of physical and mental toughness. My sister, who is three years younger than I, has always been a motivation to me. She was born with several physical disabilities and has always worn an artificial leg. She has put up with more physical pain and mental anguish than anyone I have ever met, and it has never prevented her from doing anything she has set out to do. That summer, we also spent many days at a beach on a local lake swimming, diving, and just hanging out. Terri was a good swimmer. She competed internationally. That summer she also wanted to dive off the diving boards. No easy task since she had to crawl when she had her artificial leg off. That summer, she must have made hundreds of unsuccessful attempts at diving. One day, she finally did it. You'd think this would have been enough, but she stayed with it until she pulled off a back flip. Anybody that had watched her at the beach that summer had to admire and respect what she had done. This was minor compared to all that she has accomplished in her lifetime. I hope she knows just how much I love and respect her. She has always been an inspiration to me, and I'm too much of a "Stupid Man" to tell her enough.

School started that fall, and it felt odd not to be involved in a sport. This void was replaced right away by my P.E. teacher, who was also the soccer coach. He asked me to come to practice and try out as a goalie. Soccer started after school did, so I was eligible to play it, and he knew I wasn't playing football. I had never played organized soccer before that and have never played since, but I enjoyed it immensely. I made the team as the starting JV goalie and a back up to the varsity goalie. I enjoyed soccer because it was a sport that was totally new to me and that made practice and games exciting. To this day watching soccer, live or on television, bores me to death. I appreciate the athleticism of the players, but that's about it. Fortunately, neither of my children played soccer and hopefully my grandchildren won't either. If they do, I will be supportive, but the idea of watching soccer does not thrill me.

Playing soccer also expanded my social network. I had never spent time with any of these guys before, and it was great to get to know some of the Korean kids. There were several Korean kids on the team, and they were our best players. Their skill set was well beyond that of the other players. Being a sophomore and playing a sport also caused a switch in my class schedule. I was moved to the morning classes to go to school with the juniors and seniors. Once again there was an initiation period, but nowhere near as scary as freshmen initiation. It was the varsity team that took care of this one day after practice. We returned to the locker room after practice to shower and catch the late bus home. We did this about the time the afternoon students were passing in the hallways on their way to their last class. I was the first sophomore to get the powder treatment, so I never saw this coming and was not ready to defend myself. I'm sure it would have happened anyway, as a rite of passage. I was dragged from the shower, rolled in the powder pit in the middle of the locker room, and tossed into the crowded hallway. The only way back into the locker room was to run down the hall and go out to the parking lot and enter the locker room from outside. A couple of minutes of embarrassment and it was over and the upper classmen welcomed you to the team. It was a relief to be done. I would find out later this was also a tradition on the basketball and baseball teams and every sophomore, junior, and senior on their birthdays. I have an April birthday, so I was one of the proud few that got the powder treatment four times that year. It wasn't that bad, but I'm glad schools have eliminated hazing on athletic teams today. I'm also glad there were no camera phones or YouTube in 1974-75.

RANDOM THOUGHT NUMBER TWENTY

Refer to Random Thought Number Four: I haven't changed my mind. I still want to be cremated when I die. A couple of other places I want my ashes scattered are the left hand batters' box and over the right field fence at the baseball field in Ely, Minnesota. I never hit a homerun to the opposite field, and I always enjoyed the rush of watching a ball go over the fence if I had hit it and not pitched it. I also would like to have ashes scattered on the pitchers' mound at the Bemidji State baseball field. I spent two of my favorite years of college pitching there and had a pretty good go as a Beaver playing for Bob Montebello.

My sophomore year of high school was, for the most part, a great experience. Athletically, I made the already mentioned soccer team, in the winter I played on the JV basketball team, and in the spring played on the JV baseball team. I did make one start on the varsity soccer team. Our all-state goalie came down with pink eye, and I was called up to start against the defending state champs. Coach came to one of my morning classes to give me the news so I could mentally prepare myself throughout the day... I threw up three times that day before we got on the bus to leave for the game. My shining moment was short lived. About ten minutes and two goals into the game, our opponents had a 3 on 1 breakaway. I rushed the kid with the ball as we had been coached to do to cut down on the shooting angle, but I ended up taking a knee to the head and was knocked out. That was my varsity soccer career. I did get to spend one-on-one time on the sideline with Patty McBride, our student trainer, which I parlayed into a date with a junior girl and bragging rights with sophomore soccer players. During soccer I also met my first serious girlfriend, Cathy, who was our JV manager. We continued to, I guess you would call it, go steady. That was my first long-term relationship, and it lasted until we moved again in the summer.

Making the basketball team was huge. About 150 guys were out for basketball. Cuts were made in three nights. Twelve made the varsity and fifteen were on the JV. I was blessed enough to make the JV team, one of six white kids on the two squads. Being on the basketball team reaped many benefits. Being a basketball player at Pemberton H.S. gave you rock star status. Cheerleaders were the first noticeable benefit, unfortunately not to be taken advantage of by me because Cathy was one of our statisticians and traveled with us all the time. Another benefit to being a white player on the team was that you received safe passage through the black hallway. Normally a white kid would get beat up if they were stupid enough to attempt to walk through the black hallway. We weren't segregated at the school, but every major race had their own areas in school and everyone knew it and abided by it. Being a basketball player gave you access in the white, black, and Puerto Rican hallways, but it didn't fly with the Koreans. Soccer was my pass in the Korean hallway. This allowed for a safe sophomore year as long as I did not abuse the privilege and attempt to bring a friend down one of the hallways. In the winter and spring I was never late for a class because I did not have to take alternative routes throughout the building.

Basketball road trips were pretty interesting. We played in some hostile environments. Sometimes even our JV team would get police escorts back to our seats behind the varsity bench after we showered. Our varsity upset Trenton Catholic in overtime on the road. When we got out to the bus it had been painted black. After the driver got the windows scraped off, we were about to leave when some bricks were thrown through the windows. We were given a police escort out of town. At the end of that season the state final was played between a team from Atlantic City and one of the Camden high schools. There had been a shooting when they played each other earlier in the year. The site of the championship game was changed and the location was not made public knowledge until game time to eliminate the chance of any off-court retribution.

When baseball season came up in the spring, I was jacked up like usual. I loved playing other sports, but baseball was my passion and what I lived for and excelled at. I made the team and would be pitching, catching, and playing third base as I had done since I was six. I liked playing third and catching but would have pitched every day if it was possible. I always felt like I could, but there were rules against it to protect "Stupid Men" like me.

Baseball season was going very well, but I started to have problems with my ankles. Foot and ankle problems had been a part of my life since birth, but this was different. Both ankles were beginning to lock up from time to time and took more work each time to loosen them up. I was pitching in a game when they both seized at the same time. I had to be carried off the field. My mom got an appointment scheduled with an orthopedic surgeon at Ft. Dix. He asked us to come back so I could be seen by some doctors from Temple University. On the return visit I was placed in front of this panel of doctors and went through a series of mobility exercises for them. After consulting with my mom, it was decided that immediate surgery would be needed on both ankles. I had severe calcium deposits and cartilage damage, and they wanted to try some kind of new procedure to reconstruct and fuse the ankles. The alternative was not walking in a few years. This surgery would limit mobility but give me a chance to live a normal life. The orthopedic surgeon from the base assured me I would be able to continue doing whatever I was comfortable doing, sports included. I do not know what the procedure was called, but I'm apparently among a small number of people living in the U.S. that had that surgery done. Every time I see a new orthopedic surgeon, they look at my records, get all excited, and want to dissect me. I had to stop playing that season and missed the last few weeks of school to get the surgery done. Not playing baseball tore my heart out, but a shorter school year was okay. Unfortunately, my teachers and my mom collaborated to get the rest of my work and my final exams to me so I could finish school while in the hospital.

My stay in the hospital was two weeks long—one week between ankles and one week recovering from the second ankle surgery. I had a great time in the hospital. My family visited every day, kids from school stopped in, and I got lots of sympathy from girls when Cathy wasn't around. I spent most of my time in a large ward with injured soldiers who were in basic training at Fort Dix. Many of them had injured themselves on purpose or were faking injuries to get out of basic training. The mental ward was on the floor above us and I think a lot of these guys could have qualified to go upstairs. One guy was in a complete body cast because he had jumped from a pole thinking he would sprain an ankle or break his leg. It might have been a good plan if he had landed on his feet. These guys were pretty good about not picking on me at first. My mom, much wiser than me, had told some of them that my dad was a general on the base. One day, one of my friends who was visiting let it leak that my dad was in the Navy. The pranks started immediately. They were good at it. Untying the back of my robe when I was on crutches going down the hall, peeing in my water bottle, lotion on the bed pan, which made it even more impossible to use. They would hide *Playboy* magazines under my bed and make sure my mom noticed them when she visited. All in all, pretty harmless stuff; nothing like what they would do to each other or pull on the less popular nurses and orderlies. Hopefully I will never have to spend two weeks in a hospital again, but it was a great time and much more educational than the last couple of weeks of school would have been. After leaving the hospital I was in casts and rehabbing until just before Thanksgiving.

As I said before, when we moved to New Jersey my sisters and I had no idea this was my dad's last stop in the Navy. We knew it was time for something to happen because it had been three years and we had never been anywhere more than three years. One night after supper, our parents asked us to stay at the table. They laid out brochures and *Ely Echos*, the local newspaper from Ely, Minnesota. They let us look them over for a while and then asked what we thought. My sisters and I agreed unanimously—Ely would be a great place to go on vacation. We hadn't seen our relatives in Minnesota in a few years and Duluth and Hibbing weren't far from Ely. A family reunion and a wilderness vacation would be great. Both my parents seemed almost amused when they told us that my dad was retiring from the Navy and we were moving to Ely. I'm not sure how my sisters took this news, but I was shocked—and to say the least, pissed off! I had suspected that my dad was retiring but assumed we would stay in New Jersey or somewhere near Philadelphia. The farthest I thought we would move would be Virginia Beach, Virginia. Somehow I had come to think my dad liked that area. Besides all that, I only had two years of high school left and was looking forward to playing varsity sports at Pemberton when I got out of the casts. I had a lot of friends and a girlfriend. I was not moving to Ely, Minnesota. I was a Jersey boy, and I was staying. In August, after several send-off barbecues, visits with my mom's family, and tearful goodbyes with friends, we moved to Ely. My protesting had weakened, but I still wasn't happy about it.

We made the trip to Ely in a Dodge pick-up and a camper. Instead of being in the way back of the station wagon, the premier place to ride was in the boot of the camper above the truck cab. When we arrived in Duluth/Superior, we stayed with my grandma for a couple of days. My mom and dad went up to Ely to look at houses. The next day we all went to look. We looked at a couple of places in town and a couple out of town. I remember liking one in town the most. The one my parents decided on seemed the most unlikely of all. It was about eight miles out of town on a dirt road on the White Iron Lake Chain in a place called Fall Lake Township. It was too small, with only one bathroom, not enough bedrooms, no garage, and it was in the middle of nowhere. I thought we had reached nowhere when we first pulled into Ely, but apparently you weren't in nowhere until you drove out of the other end of town. The house did have running water, but it was pumped up from the lake. I couldn't help but think who does that? The house was heated by a wood-burning furnace, and again, who does that? I don't know how they arrived at the decision to buy this house. I had a lot of respect for my dad, but I was beginning to wonder if he might be crazy or the most "Stupid Man" on the planet. He was not only moving his family from New Jersey to what might be the very edge of civilization, he seemed to be genuinely excited about it. We stopped at the Realtor's office in Ely, and my parents took care of whatever business needed to be completed.

Before we left Ely that day, we stopped at the Dairy Queen. This was and is still today Ely's only fast food restaurant. I talked earlier in the book about walking into Saquoit to cash in "soda" bottles until I learned otherwise upon moving to Minnesota in 1975.

This was the day. When we were giving our orders at the Dairy Queen, I ordered a medium soda and waited for the girl behind the counter to ask me what kind. She asked me to repeat my order. Once again I said a medium soda. She left the counter and went to talk to someone in the back. She came back and said, "We do not have soda." I pointed to the soda fountain machine and asked if it was broke. She informed me that the machine I was referring to was a "pop" machine and if I wanted a pop, they did have that, but no soda. I like my Coke products, so from that day forward it has been "pop." I would find out later that there are many other words unique to Ely and the Iron Range. We returned to my grandma's that night to finish packing what we had with us to move up to Ely. My grandma was going to come live with us for a while also. I figured for sure this meant I would be sleeping in the camper or outside on the ground.

RANDOM THOUGHT NUMBER TWENTY ONE

I bought a new cell phone a couple of days ago. My old one was starting to act up, and they don't make parts for it anymore. The salesperson said I was eligible for an upgrade. She showed me several phones and suggested a smart phone. I told her I needed a phone that I could make calls from and that would receive calls. I do not text, I don't need to access the internet, I don't need apps or a GPS, and I do not need to take pictures or videos with my phone. Eventually, she found one that fit my needs. You'd think I had asked for a couple of soup cans attached by a string, but I knew a smart phone was out of the question. I still won't buy Smartwater because I haven't figured out how to open the bottles. So I now have a new cell phone and hope I can figure out how to operate it before summer is over.

My dad obviously had vision I was not blessed with. Within the next two years we added two stories to the side of the house and extended the walkout basement. We also built a three-stall garage. Before any of this took place, we had built an outhouse. In Ely, I guess that would mean we had one and a half bathrooms. It didn't take long to see what had drawn my dad to Ely. It seemed like every day I found something else about the town, the surrounding area, the people, and the way of life that I began liking more every day. Living at the lake was great, especially after I found out you could drive in Minnesota when you were 16 and I was not going to have to wait to turn 17. This was the one thing that made my friends in New Jersey jealous. Nothing else I told them about Ely ever made any sense to them.

I think school had already been in session for a couple of days when we went to enroll. My first meeting was with the principal, and then I went to the guidance counselor to schedule my classes. After that I was introduced to a student who showed me around the school and tried to answer any questions I could think of. Ely High School had three floors and no working elevator that my tour guide knew of, so the tour took a while because I was still on crutches and in two walking casts from the ankle surgeries. When Earl, my student tour guide, asked if I had any questions, I had a few. First, what do you guys do for fun? His answer: cruise Sheridan Street, ride around the lake and drink beer, and play hockey. Second question: how is the basketball team? Answer: I don't know. Earl was a hockey player. Third question: how are the girls here? Answer: there are a few, but the Babbitt girls are better. Next question: how is the baseball team? Answer: great! Earl was a baseball player. The last question—the one that had been on my mind since I arrived, other than when is lunch—was are the lockers being painted? Earl looked confused. I would later learn this was a natural state for him.

He asked me why I would think that. I was wondering because some of the lockers were partially open and none of the lockers had locks on them. Earl asked, "Why would we have locks on our lockers?" I said, "So nobody steals your stuff." Earl said, "We borrow from each other, but nobody steals each other's stuff here." I would later learn that nobody in Ely locked their cars or houses, either. I gained an instant appreciation for Ely because the people trusted each other and had a deep sense of security.

The next several days at school were great. The kids were really friendly and wanted to talk. The question I got tired of answering was: "What happened to your legs?" For my own amusement, I started making things up. I told some kids I was in a car accident, jumped off the Atlantic City pier, had a skydiving accident, and—my personal favorite—my dad had some serious gambling debts with the Mob. I was pretty proud of myself. They seemed to buying it. I was meeting and talking to new kids every day. Years later, one of my closest friends told me the reason everyone wanted to talk to me had nothing to do with my legs being in casts, they just wanted to hear the New Jersey/Philadelphia accent.

RANDOM THOUGHT NUMBER TWENTY TWO

I take offense when someone calls me "Turnbull" instead of using my first name or putting "Mr." or "Coach" in front of it. I try not to call people by their last name because I think it is demeaning. You are not recognizing a person's individual identity when you just use the last name. I have one exception to this rule. My father-in-law calls me "Turnbull." He can call me whatever he wants. I am married to his daughter, and I owe him a lot of money.

The more I got to know people in Ely, the more I envied them and wanted to be accepted. There was a sense of community I had never really experienced before. Some of the kids I met had lived there all their lives. I had never lived anywhere for more than three years. When you talked to older people it was pretty obvious that if you weren't third generation, you were not from Ely or anywhere on the Iron Range for that matter. It also seemed like everyone had a nickname: Boobs, Junco, Seep, Ram, Patch, Ruts, Scoffer, Squish, Hench, Bear, Moaner, Pod, Beets, Mona, Jaggy, Cheeks, Toes, Tat, Thatch, Toot, Spoon, Clyde, Goth, Gobi, Jeep, Toots, Hot Rod, Rocket, and so on. I wanted an Ely nickname.

I already had nicknames in my past. I was Little Michael in my mom's family, because my Uncle Mike was Big Michael. The black guys on my basketball team at Pemberton High School called me Silky or Smooth. That was all in the past; now I wanted an Ely nickname. I didn't make this public knowledge, but I felt it would be some show of acceptance. It happened—the nickname was Buckles. I only hear it when I'm in Ely or run into people from Ely somewhere else. It is an all-star wrestling reference to coming off the top turnbuckle and also a play on my last name.

I was still in casts until a few days before Thanksgiving, so I spent that first fall in Ely going to school, doing whatever I could do around the house, cruising Sheridan Street, and riding around Sahrawi Lake when I got the opportunity. I also went to football games, home and away—there was always a fan bus for away games. Our football team was good, especially the senior class. Ely was still in the Iron Range Conference at that time and competed well with the big schools, such as, Grand Rapids, Hibbing, and Virginia. When I was watching football, all I could think of was getting my casts off and hopefully rehabbing in time to play basketball and baseball later that year.

In late November I had an appointment with an orthopedic surgeon at St. Luke's Hospital in Duluth. My wish came true. It was time for the last casts to come off. I had been in casts for a little over six months, so I was more than ready for the last ones to come off. I'll admit, I have skinny legs (my Aunt Kathy calls them Turnbull legs), but I couldn't believe the amount of atrophy. I told the doctor it was going to be a lot of work to get into basketball shape. His response was to forget sports and just be happy I could walk. I was crushed at first and then became angry. My surgeon in New Jersey had said I could attempt whatever I wanted to. My new doctor eventually agreed to let me give it a try. Coach Marsnik and my new teammates were very patient and encouraging with me. Coach did a great job putting me through rehab drills and even arranged time in the pool for me. The rehab was slow and steady. I spent most of my time on the B-Squad and eventually started logging some varsity minutes, enough to earn a varsity letter. I was proud to get that first varsity letter and an Ely Timberwolves letter jacket.

Spring was even better. Spring hits Ely in May, but they start calling it spring in April. I had never spent so much time practicing baseball in a gym my entire life. Physically, I was feeling completely recovered from the ankle surgeries and was hoping I could have an impact on the success of the baseball team. I won a starting job at third base and was one of the top three pitchers. We had a great year but eventually lost to Babbitt-Embarrass in the district championship. Babbitt had a good team, and they went on to win the state championship.

I also got my driver's license that spring, still ahead of schedule with my friends in New Jersey but a year behind by Minnesota standards. Being able to drive myself in to town and cruise Sheridan in my parents' Country Squire was great. I tricked out the station wagon right away. I went to Radio Shack and bought a cassette player you could plug into the lighter. I put it on the front seat and moved it to the floor if I got lucky enough to have a girl next to me. The other thing I had to learn that hadn't been taught in drivers' education was the one-fingered wave. You drove with one hand on top of the steering wheel and if you passed someone you knew, you raised your index finger. If you passed someone strange you just nodded your head, chin up. (This is pretty much unique to Ely, but

I have noticed the same practice on occasion from farmers on back roads in southern Minnesota.)

Summer is by far the best time of the year in Ely, and the first summer we lived there was no exception. Now I could see why my dad wanted a house on the lake, with unlimited access to swimming, canoeing, and fishing. Our house was on the Kawishiwi River between White Iron, Farm, and Garden Lakes. You could travel for miles by motorboat until the BWCA was expanded and motor restrictions went in. Other than cutting and splitting countless cords of wood, life at the lake was great. I also had a maintenance job with parks and recreation. My duties were mostly cutting grass at the cemetery, painting at Semer's Park, and grooming the baseball field. I also played a lot of American Legion baseball, and we had a summer basketball league. Free time was mostly spent chasing girls, playing pool and drinking beer at Silver Rapids Lodge, and hanging out at Petrichs' cabin on Fall Lake. Cruising Sheridan Street and harassing swampies, a local term for tourists, was a popular activity also. Unless the swampies were teenage girls, then we put on the local charm. Babbitt had Peter Mitchell Days, which were worth a couple of road trips. Ely's big summer event was the 4th of July. Great parade and Sheridan Street was packed for it. That's still true today; Whiteside Park fills with people, and there are plenty of games and food booths. Various races highlight the games, and it seemed like it was always an Anderson kid winning the races. The fireworks at night are some of the best on the Iron Range. On truly special occasions, when we could pool enough money together, a bunch of us guys would take a road trip to Virginia or Duluth. I saw my third and fourth concerts in Duluth, Gordon Lightfoot both times.

Summer passes way too quickly in northern Minnesota, and school started again. I had decided with the help of Coach Mischke that football wasn't going to be in the mix because my ankles just weren't up to it. This gave me more time to get ready for basketball, and I still went to all the football games. It was Ely's last year in the Iron Range conference, and it was a tough year. I also became a volleyball fan. Compared to the volleyball that is played today, it was terrible. You see better junior high volleyball in Minnesota today. It wasn't so much that I was a volleyball fan; my main goal was to meet the manager. Her name was Pam Loe, and I had to find a way to meet her.

I started to do my research on Pam. My players today would

call it stalking or creeping. I call it getting to know as much about someone as you can before you actually meet them. I didn't want anything to go wrong. I couldn't rely on being the new kid in town thing anymore, as I had lived in Ely for a year now. I found out she was a junior and went to the Methodist church. I had always dated Catholics, but this would have to be overlooked. Besides, the Methodist church was right next to St. Anthony's Catholic Church. She worked at Britton's Café and the movie theater and was very involved at school. Pam was in the band, student council, football and hockey cheerleading, played basketball, and was the volleyball manager. She was also smart. Her dad owned R&R Transfer and worked in the mine. Her mom, according to some of my friends, was a nice lady but strict. Pam had two younger brothers. She lived somewhere on Harvey Street, and her best friend was Jean. Her uncle was Jeep, and he ran a Canoe Outfitting business in town and Prairie Portage on Moose Lake. Pam's dad and Uncle Jeep both were rumored to be pretty tough guys to deal with. With all this newfound knowledge, I didn't lose sight of the fact that she was one of the best looking girls in school and I had to meet her and ask her out. The worst that could happen would be she would break my heart and say "No." It was obvious to me that she was special and probably had high standards, so I would have to put my best foot forward and not let her see right away that I had the potential to be a "Stupid Man."

I continued to build up my confidence before approaching her. I should be confident; I got good grades, college was in my future, I played two varsity sports, I was a good looking guy, I was a bus boy at Vertins' Restaurant, still had the New Jersey accent working, was still very new to town by Ely standards, and I drove a Country Squire station wagon with a tape player that plugged into the lighter. The Country Squire wasn't so cool, but the tape player was. Also, I had recently received another stamp of approval from my peers and had been chosen a fall homecoming king candidate. I had no chance of winning, but I was in the running! I hung around after volleyball matches and offered to help with whatever I could while I struck up a conversation. Things were going well, but she never did let me help with anything. I learned later this was because she hadn't had time to train me in on exactly how she wanted it done. Thirty-five years later I'm starting to get it; I can help after she has had time to properly train me in. If not, I just stay out of the way.

There was a Tuesday night home volleyball match, and I was

planning on leaving on Thursday to visit colleges with my friend Mike. The homecoming dance was the following weekend, so I had to ask her to the dance now. I followed her around after the match as she cleaned up. I think she let me carry a pole this time. I saw that as a good sign and asked her to the dance. She said yes, but I would have to meet her mom and dad first to see what they thought.

RANDOM THOUGHT NUMBER TWENTY THREE

There is a statewide promotion going on in Minnesota this summer. It is a campaign to not move firewood in order to keep some beetle from spreading. There are radio and television commercials for it and billboards on highways promoting the idea, all with people saying, "I promise not to move firewood." There are now new advertisements asking people to burn firewood where you purchase it. I hope people don't buy into this idea because if they do, there are going to be a lot of Holiday gas station stores and offices at state parks in Minnesota burning down. Am I the only "Stupid Man" in Minnesota struggling with this? I'm not taking the oath until I get the details.

Mike and I left on Thursday to visit colleges in St. Cloud and the Twin Cities. We visited St. John's, St. Thomas, and the University of Minnesota. I loved them all. I wanted to go to St. John's, but my parents thought otherwise when they saw what the tuition was. They said I should think about state schools and not to forget Vermilion Community College right there in Ely. I was later recruited to play baseball at St. Cloud State and UM-Duluth and did official visits. Mike and I spent three nights at his Uncle Larry's who was in law school at William Mitchell College in St. Paul. Other than having to spend part of one night in the student lounge with Larry and other law students watching the Jimmy Carter and Gerald Ford presidential debate, we had a great time. Mike and I got dressed up in our leisure suits because Larry took us to some of the higher end bars and strip clubs in Minneapolis-St. Paul. This was also my first time out on Hennepin Avenue. The last night out we ended up playing football on Hennepin Avenue with some business executives after the bars closed. My leisure suit got ripped, and that was a hard one to explain to my mom when we got home. Too bad—or luckily, depending on who's looking at it—we were only allowed three college visits that counted as excused absences from school. I had more on my mind than choosing a college right away. I had to get home and find out when I was meeting Pam's parents.

RANDOM THOUGHT NUMBER TWENTY FOUR

I coach women's volleyball at Hibbing Community College. I love this part of my job and take great pride in the success of our program. We start practice in two days and are looking forward to another successful season. Tonight I received an email from my sophomore middle hitter, a projected starter, apologizing because she has decided she can't play this year. She needs to concentrate on her nursing classes. I agree with that, but do you think she could have decided this a few months ago, when I had time to recruit another middle hitter? Hopefully one of our incoming freshmen will step up. I have to go home and try to sleep now. Just have to roll with it.

Sometime in the middle of the week it was show time! Pam's dad wasn't there right away, so I spent time talking to her mom. Nice lady—she didn't grill me nearly as bad as I had imagined. It turned out that she was friends with Mike's mom and had already checked up on me. Geraldine, Mike's mom, had spoken well of me. I also met Pam's younger brothers, and Mike, the youngest, was pretty talkative. Pat couldn't have cared less. The dog, Gigi, seemed to like me. When her dad showed up he wasn't in the best of moods. Something had happened at the warehouse, and he needed to get some sleep before going to work at the mine. My first encounter with Rod was brief, but he did think it was okay to take Pam to the dance if the dog liked me. Good thing, because I had no backup plan. Anyway, I was definitely excited about having my first date with Pam.

RANDOM THOUGHT NUMBER TWENTY FIVE

I have a sign on the outside of my office door that reads, "I have gone to find myself. If I get here before I return, keep me here. I'll be back shortly."

Pam dances very well and enjoys it. I on the other hand don't, but I do enjoy watching people dance. I managed, like usual, to stumble my way through it as long as we could get a few slow dances in. All in all it was a good night. We left on time to get a couple of quick cruises on Sheridan Street before I had to have her home. We talked outside on the back step for a while. I thought I might get a kiss goodnight, but Tootsie, her mom, flashed the porch light a couple of times and that put an abrupt end to the night. That first kiss would have to wait. We would be going out again.

RANDOM THOUGHT NUMBER TWENTY SIX

I just got done inflating fifty volleyballs for the first day of practice. I have always wondered what would happen if you did not moisten the needle before inflating.

The rest of my senior year was great. Pam and I continued going out, quickly moving to exclusive. At some point, Pam's mom started waiting a little longer to flip the porch light on, and we had that first kiss.

Basketball season went very well. I was a starter, and we made it to the District 27 semi-final before losing to Eveleth at Miners' Memorial Arena in Virginia. Eveleth went on and lost to a very good Silver Bay team that ended up going to the state tournament.

Baseball ended as my junior year had with a district final loss to Babbitt. Babbitt advanced to the state tournament again but did not win the state title this time. In both my junior and senior years, we struggled with Babbitt during the high school season, but seemed to have no trouble with them during the American Legion season.

RANDOM THOUGHT NUMBER TWENTY SEVEN

A nasty rumor started around Hibbing a couple of years ago. This rumor was started by Bob Nyberg. I like Bob; he is a good guy. I played baseball against Bob in high school when he played for Hibbing and I played for Ely. Bob had a great career at Hibbing. I work with Bob's wife Kathy, a nice lady. I have had the pleasure of coaching two of his daughters, Nicole and Weezer. I also have coached his future son-in-law Matt, all great kids. Bob insists he hit a homerun off me in high school in a game in Ely. I'll admit, I gave up my share of homeruns over the years, but I have researched the newspaper clippings my mom saved and could find nothing about Bob's alleged homerun in Ely off me. I did find out that I threw a one-hitter in Hibbing and it was Bob who had the one hit. I will always credit him for that, but I will not perpetuate the homerun story.

At the end of my senior year I did receive offers to play at Saint Cloud State and the University of Minnesota, Duluth. I also had a chance to go back to New Jersey and play at Trenton State College for the guy who had been my JV coach at Pemberton Township. Truth be told, I was in love, and Pam was a year younger than me. Staying in Ely, attending Vermilion Community College, and playing baseball and basketball seemed to be a better option. Besides, I had only lived in Ely for a little less than two years and didn't have the burning desire a lot of other classmates had to leave right away.

Pam had me doing some things I otherwise wouldn't have experienced. She was involved in dance, ballet, band, pageants, figure skating, and school plays. All were events that I would most likely have never attended if not for her. On the other hand, I don't know how much basketball or baseball she would have watched if not for me. She was also not much for partying, which was a good thing. Because of her I was a much more focused student-athlete my senior year. Not a saint, but definitely a lot more subdued than my junior year.

About midway through my senior year, I was called in to see Mr. Peninger after school. Mr. Peninger was our senior social problems teacher and class advisor. Mr. Peninger ended up challenging my Catholic faith a little bit but definitely opened my mind to a new concept. He was convinced I had a poltergeist. He told me I should not be scared. He was convinced it was a playful one and was just messing with me. He pointed out some things he had witnessed that convinced him this was true. He was watching one day when I was hanging out on the top floor and leaning on the stairway rail. I bumped my books with my elbow and they fell to the second floor and hit Miss Jaksha in the head. I had brushed it off as a random act of bad luck. On another day Gotch and I were walking behind Miss Gourley in the hallway. I ran up to her and pretended to kick her in the butt. Unfortunately she dropped a pencil, stopped and bent over to pick it up, and I ended up really kicking her. After we picked her and her stuff up, she grabbed Gotch by the ear and whisked him off to the office. He tried to defend himself but Miss Gourley said, "Michael would have never done that!" I let Gotch take the fall because he owed me one. I had saved him from getting beat up by Joe Shere in the locker room during basketball season. Again, I had considered it a freak accident, but Mr. Peninger saw it differently.

He went on to point out two other things that had happened in class. In economics we were reviewing that day's *Wall Street Journal.* We all had the same paper. Mine had one problem—no New York Stock Exchange. Other than that it was the same as everyone else's, including page numbers in the same sequence. There was no way to explain this logically. When our graduation announcements and invitations came in, I was the only one who did not receive theirs in the whole senior class. The invoice indicated all my materials had been shipped from Jostens but they were not in any of the boxes. Mr. Peninger definitely had my attention now. The clincher was that I had been assigned a research project for missing class. He had an open room next to his classroom, where he stored old *Newsweek, US News and World Reports,* and *Time* magazines. If we missed class he would give us a question to research and in the process we would organize the magazines according to date. I remember my question was to find the profit margin of the Chiquita Banana Company in 1957. I researched it for days. I never did find the answer but organized most of the storage room. When Mr. Peninger checked, the room was in total disarray. The magazines were less organized than ever before. Being a stubborn "Stupid Man," I was close but not completely sold on this poltergeist concept. The conversation ended when Mr. Peninger pointed out the aura he had noticed hovering around me several times. I left the room with a whole new view of life and random happenings.

Soon the time had come, time to graduate from Ely Memorial High School as a full-fledged Timberwolf. Pam and I had gone to the prom (my first and her second), awards night, junior/senior tea, and yearbook signing. I don't remember who the keynote speaker was or what the class motto or final song from the choir was. I am pretty sure the class of 1977 was the last class to graduate on a flat stage. Every class after us was placed on choir risers. It might have had something to do with the empty quart vodka bottle that rolled slowly from the back of the stage and off the front, crashing into the orchestra pit and disrupting the keynote address. Any one of us sitting in the back knew where it came from and why it was empty.

The graduation ceremonies continued and all 99 of us received our diplomas and were sent on our way.

One more summer before entering the new world of college, and I had things to do. The first line of business was to sell the car my parents had given me for graduation. I'm still convinced this was a devious trick my dad had played on me. It was a Pontiac GTO and needed a lot of work, well beyond my mechanical and body work skills. I'm sure the intent was to make one more attempt to do work on a car and possibly learn some life skills. I did enough to it with help from friends and my dad to get it fixed up enough to sell. After it sold, I replaced it with Larry Grahek's 1965 Galaxie for $500. I figured if Larry made it to the major leagues I could sell it for big money. Talented as he was, Larry never made the big club, but the car got me to my first year of teaching. I worked for parks and recreation again but strictly at the baseball field; seniority has its perks. I also got a job at Kat's Liquor as a clerk and stocker. What a great job! Len and Pat were great people to work for and kept me on through college and a couple of summers after I was teaching. I also got to work with some great people: Grandma Katauskas, Joe, Hitch, Lucy, Pete, and Konrad. I have a lot of fond memories, like hiding in the cooler to catch shoplifters, carding kids after they paid and keeping their money, delivering to Jakich's Bar, seeing how many cases we could carry, and taste testing Hamm's Pony Kegs. I also got to meet Haystack Calhoun in the store one day and on another night that guy who played the really smart detective on the Barney Miller television show.

The highlight of the summer was hosting the American Legion state baseball tournament. We played more games than any other Ely Legion team ever played in preparing to play in the tournament. We played what seemed like all week long every week, a couple of mid-week Border Area games, and tournaments on weekends. In between Legion games, I would play for the Blue Sox, our local town team. I would only play in out of town games and if I pitched I was placed on the roster as Oscar Swanson in the box score. Coach Marsnik, our Legion coach, didn't want us pitching if we played with the Blue Sox. Oscar was out of town at the time so it all worked out. We represented Ely well at the state tournament. We defeated Morton the first morning. In the night cap we got no-hit by Jim Eisenrich's Saint Cloud team. We came back the next day and lost a close game to Arcade Phalen from St. Paul.

My cousin Eugene and a couple of his friends drove from

Philadelphia to Ely to visit for a week. I showed them all that Ely had to offer: fishing, wood splitting, road trips, cruising Sheridan Street, driving around Shagawa Lake, Petrich's cabin, and drinking beer and playing pool at Silver Rapid's Lodge. We topped it off with a couple of stops at the Dairy Queen. They loved it, but also pointed out a couple of things I had forgotten about the East Coast. We were on a road trip one night to Virginia and stopped along the road somewhere. Eugene asked where we were. I told him, "Nowhere." He said, "We have to be somewhere." I said, "We are just in the woods between Tower and Virginia." Eugene said, "You still have to be somewhere. At home in Philadelphia you are always somewhere." Personally, I now appreciate the fact that we can drive to nowhere in northern Minnesota. On another night we were sitting out on our dock and Eugene and his friends wanted to know what the odd smell was. We eliminated lake, water, and trees. Eventually I figured it out. It was fresh air they smelled for the first time. I had forgotten the smell of the city, the oil refineries by the river, and the salt air at the shore in New Jersey. Today, I don't miss city or oil refinery smells, but anytime I get to the ocean I enjoy the smell of the ocean air as I approach the coast.

With college and adulthood on the horizon, I was ready to answer the question, "Where are you from?" The answer: I am from Ely, Minnesota. I know this to be true because every time Tom Coombe mentions my name in the *Ely Echo* since I have moved away, before my name he writes, "Ely native." As far as the question, "Where did you grow up?" I'm still a work in progress.

RANDOM THOUGHT NUMBER TWENTY EIGHT

I teach a wellness class at Hibbing Community College. Today we discussed methods of reducing stress or things to do to relax. I get relaxed any time I'm near a body of water, especially the ocean. I am definitely an amateur, but I also enjoy fishing. For me, it is not about how much fish you catch; it is about getting out on a nice day on the lake and just fishing and relaxing. I also enjoy doing manual labor outside, especially things you don't have to think about. I call them no brain activities, like cutting the grass, splitting wood, raking leaves, and blowing or shoveling snow. My favorite man tools are leaf blowers and snow blowers. There is something about moving stuff around with the force of air that I get a kick out of. I know my neighbor Brian is jealous because he doesn't have a leaf blower and I got a new snow blower from my wife last Christmas.

RANDOM THOUGHT NUMBER TWENTY NINE

I love hot weather, short mild winters, and the ocean. So, as a "Stupid Man," when I retire, whenever that may be, Pam and I plan to move to Ely. This is where I plan to finish growing up and Pam and I can grow old together at the end of the road. My mom and dad moved our family to Ely in 1975. My dad had only been to Ely once for about half an hour when he was eighteen years old and was on leave from the Navy. Before my dad died in 1989 he told me he always knew he would return to Ely. He said you either love it or hate it. There is no in between. I, like my dad, learned to love it, and I'm going back when the time is right. I pray I will get to spend more than fourteen years there.

1981-82 Lake Park Parkers Boys' Basketball Seniors [Lake Park, MN]
First basketball team I coached. We won the school's first ever District 23A Championship
Back Row: L-R: Eric Hendrickson, Jeff Kamstra, Scott Elder, Bruce Roen, Scott Ebersole, and Barry Nelson
Front Row: L-R: Rodney Savig, Coach Mike Turnbull, and Darrel Pederson

1991-92 Wadena- Deer Creek Volleyball Team [Wadena, MN]
This was Wadena-Deer Creek's first team to qualify for the Minnesota State Tournament
Back Row L-R: Jacki Uselman, Naomi White, Kelly Johnson, Missy Becker, Kristina Haraldson, Michelle Clark, Missy Pickar, Michelle McKellep, and Jody Pearson. *Front Row L-R:* Coach Mike Turnbull, Rhonda Birch, Hally Damm, Steph Jessop, Ann Kaatz, and Lexie Turnbull

1977 American Legion Baseball Team Ely, MN [First day of State Tournament]
Back Row L-R: Mike Petrich, Goose Gornick, Matty Yernatich, Mike Turnbull, Walt Passi, Randy Skube, Curt Hartleben, and Coach George Marsnik
Middle Row L-R: Dennis Minier, Mike Jamnick, John Jamnick, Darryl Salo, Pete Marsnik, and Jodi Bach
Front Row L-R: Sara Marsnik and Tom Coombe
*This was the first time Ely and Tower-Soudan combined for American Legion Baseball. Gornick, Yernatich, Passi, and Mike Jamnick were all from Tower-Soudan.

1975-76 Ely High School Basketball Team [My junior year, first year living in Ely]
Back Row L-R: Assistant Coach Ackerman, Hank Tjader, Mark Nelson, John Podominick, Pete Scheuer, Jeff Anderson, and Coach George Marsnik.
Middle Row L-R: Tim Anderson, Bob Marolt, Joe Shere, Keith Rhein, and Mike Hren
Front Row L-R: Brian Chase, Dave Gotchnik, Pete Marsnik, Mike Turnbull, and Karl Scheuer

Mike Turnbull [Pitching for Bemidji State University / Bemidji, MN 1980]

Mike Turnbull warming up in the bull pen before a game at Mankato State University. [1981]
I don't know what I was smiling about; Mankato was tougher than hell!

1999-2000 Hibbing CC Men's Basketball Team
Picture was taken at Kevin McHale Day at the Hibbing Memorial Building in Hibbing, MN
Minnesota Timberwolves mascot "Crunch" is doing the dunking.
I'm sure he wasn't the first one to dunk on us that year.

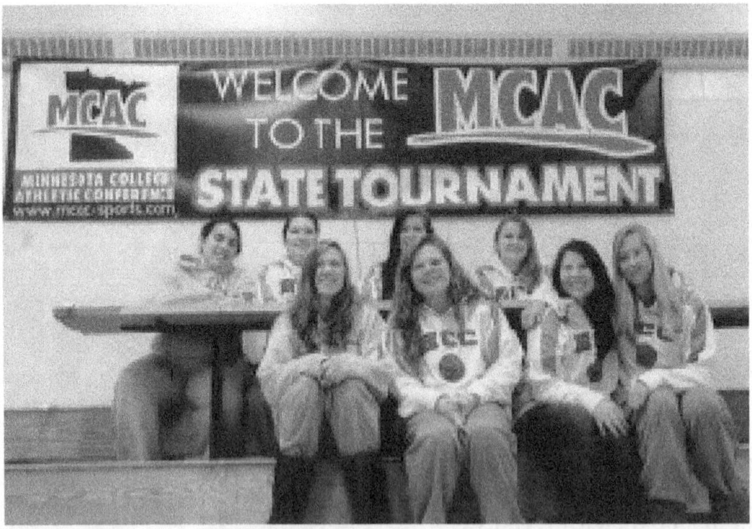

Hibbing CC Women's Basketball Team [Proud bunch of Cardinals. February 26, 2011, shortly after defeating Mesabi in the State quarter finals.]
Back Row L-R: Andrea Becker, Kasey Palmer, Whitney Finco, and Natalie Stine
Front Row L-R: Jenna Zmyslony, Kiersten Apel, Brittany Paige, and Melissa Nyberg

Fall 2007 [Mike Turnbull]
One of my volleyball players asked me to stop in front of Jay Leno on a TV screen.

Coach Mike Turnbull and Captains
L-R: Ashley Palmer and Lindsay Jacobson
2008 National NJCAA Volleyball Tournament Banquet.
[2008 Hibbing CC Volleyball]

2008 NJCAA National Volleyball Tournament / Hibbing CC 3rd Place
L-R: Samantha Lindfors, Breanna Chamernick, Daisha VanOverbeke, Lindsay Jacobson, Mike Turnbull, Ashley Palmer, Erianne Bright, Krystal Ramfjord, Kelly Hams, and Brittany Easley.

August 2009: Traditional event for Hibbing CC Volleyball teams.
Mash Potato Wrestling at the Annual Potato Days Festival in Barnesville, MN.

Coach Mike Turnbull: 2000 Hibbing CC Volleyball.
The theme for the season was "Winners under Construction."

Another "Intense moment" with the 2007 Hibbing CC Volleyball team.
L-R: Lindsay Jacobson, Laura Girard, Sarah Bailey, Mike Turnbull, Michelle Barron, Carrie Kozumplik, Karla Elgin, Nina Lutmer, and Dana Anderson.

Mike and Blaine Turnbull after Blaine's last game as a sophomore at Hibbing CC [2005]

2004-2005 Hibbing CC Men's Basketball Sophomores
Back Row L-R: Jimmy Howard, Aaron Turner, Luke Carlson, Coach Mike Turnbull, and Blaine Turnbull
Front L-R: Corey Shephard and Dan Helstrom

Hibbing CC Spring Baseball Trip 2008 Miami, OK. [Mike Turnbull]

Hibbing CC practice baseball field May 7, 2010.
We played four games in Hibbing the next day to finish the season.

Hibbing CC Spring Baseball trip 2004. Fayetteville, SC.
A storm had knocked the roof off the dugout the night before.

Side trip on Hibbing CC Baseball 2000 spring trip. [Dyersville, IA]

2001 Hibbing CC spring baseball trip. Orlando, FL. [Mike Turnbull]
It was a wig!

1999 Hibbing CC spring baseball trip. Florida/Alabama border.

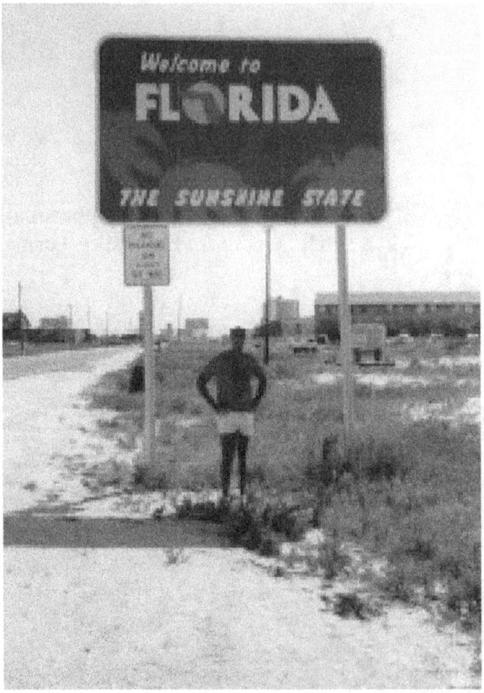

1989 Mike Turnbull [Yes that is the same place as the previous picture]

June 12, 1982 Mike & Pam's wedding
Back Row L-R: Pat Loe, Mike Loe, Tim Milliard [Milly], Pete Marsnik, Mike Turnbull, Mike Petrich, Ed Nordskog [Eddy], Jim Grim [Grimmer], and Lance Chambers [Lanny]
Middle Row L-R: Betsy Loushin, Jean Bauman, Pam [Loe] Turnbull, Lynn Bassett, and Amy McDougall

Front Row L-R: Mindy LaTourell, Mitch Hueman, and Missy LaTourell

June 12, 1982 Mike & Pam's wedding
Left: Rod and Tootsie Loe
Middle: Mike and Pam Turnbull
Right: Jack and Pat Turnbull

My mom and dad's 25th Wedding Anniversary [Patricia & Jack Turnbull]

Mike Turnbull & daughter Lexie
A little father daughter time before my sister Lisa's wedding.

1999 Mike Turnbull chilling on a snorkeling boat in Maui.
Back Left: Sister Terri Turnbull, brother in-law Jeff Jennings, and sister Stacie Jennings.
Front Right: Daughter Lexie Turnbull

1999: my sister Stacie's wedding in Maui.
My dad passed away in 1989 so I had the honor of walking my sister Stacie and my mom Patricia up the aisle.

My dad Jack Turnbull
Chief Petty Officer U.S. Navy

1987: My dad and my children Blaine and Lexie.
Sad to say, but the only grandchildren he saw born before he passed in 1989.

Spring 1987
Mike, Pam, Lexie, and Blaine Turnbull

Summer 1981 Engagement picture
Pam [Loe] Turnbull and Mike Turnbull

1985-86 school year Lake Park H.S. Lake Park, MN
I've never kept a tidy office. [Mike Turnbull]

1981-82 school year.
Lake Park H.S. Lake Park, MN
First teaching and coaching job after college [Mike Turnbull]

1982-83 school year Lake Park H.S. Lake Park, MN
Kids have put up with my sloppy writing for 31 years now. [Mike Turnbull]

Summer 1989 somewhere in Alabama
I'll admit it: I "borrowed" the little sign. It is still in my basement if someone wants it back. [Mike Turnbull]

Summer 1989 Gulf Shores, AL
First time at the Pink Pony. I love that place! [Mike Turnbull]

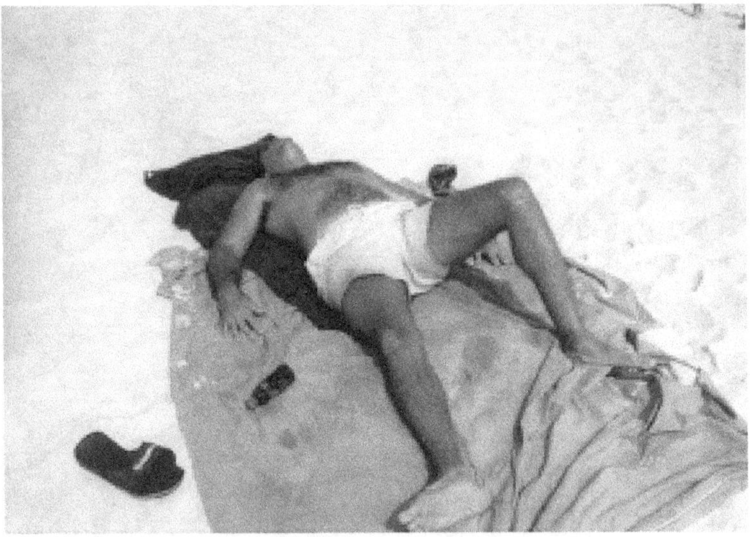

Summer 1989 Gulf Shores, AL
Some pictures tell it all; flat feet, skinny "Turnbull legs," and hairy. Definitely not easy to look at, but I do love the beach! [Mike Turnbull]

Summer 2011 Omaha, NE [TD Ameritrade Park]
Blaine and Mike Turnbull at College World Series
[First year at TD Ameritrade Park]

ELY ECHO FOR AUG. 17, 1977, PAGE 11

DETERMINATION—Ely's Mike Turnbull grimaces as he fires a curve ball against Morton last weekend in the State Legion Tournament. It was the second time in three years that Ely hosted the event.

August 17, 1977 Ely, MN
Mike Turnbull pitching against Morton in American Legion Minnesota State Baseball Tournament. I will never forget how good I always felt on a pitcher's mound.

If you were to write a book, what would it be about?

Mike Turnbull: My Dad was in the navy and we traveled a lot so it would probably be about all the places I've been and all the screwy people I've met along the way. The screwy people are the best kind to be with.

Fall 1977 [From Vermilion Communit College newspaper] Ely, MN
Question of the day: WHO KNEW?

District boys' basketball tournament [VS- Glyndon-Felton at Concordia College in Moorhead, MN March 6, 1986.]
Reads: Coach Mike Turnbull of Lake Park showed signs of pressure in final seconds Tuesday night. [Detriot Lakes Tribune - Thursday, March 6, 1986]

Hibbing CC Women's Basketball February 26, 2011
State MCAC quarter-finals, preparing to take on Mesabi CC.

Summer 2010 Omaha, NE College World Series
Mike Turnbull mugging it up for the Ely Echo in front of Rosenblatt Stadium.
The last summer the CWS was held at Rosenblatt.

February 25, 2011 taken at MCAC Women's State Tournament Banquet
I've never looked so smart. Must have been deep into another "RANDOM THOUGHT OF A STUPID MAN."

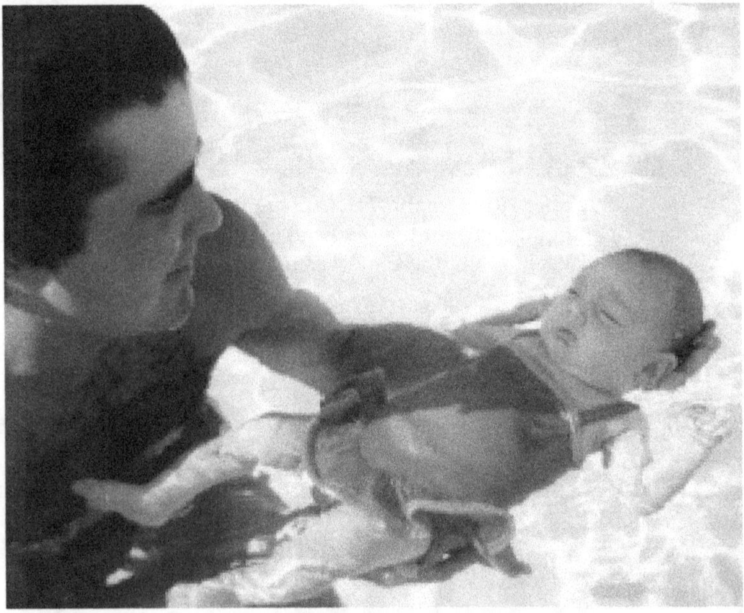

July 1983 City Pool Lake Park, MN
Mike Turnbull & Daughter Lexie [Lexie is 2 ½ months old]. I make reference to this on page 69 of the manuscript in Chapter 4. [Last paragraph page 69] It was a mommy and me swimming class. I was teaching the class, but Pam wanted me to be the mommy also. Turned out to be an unforgettable parenting experience.

1984 Lake Park, MN The Ode family

L-R: Jana, Becky, Jody, and Bud Ode

If not for the guidance and friendship of the Odes, I really don't know if I would have made it through my first years of teaching and coaching and I'm sure Pam and I would have struggled a lot more trying to start a marriage and later raising two young children. We were clueless, me much more so than Pam.

Mitchell-Tappan House Bed & Breakfast Hibbing, MN March 28, 2011
I know the website says owned and operated by Pam and
Mike Turnbull, but believe me Pam is definitely the CEO.

CHAPTER TWO

COLLEGE

I would like to tell you I had a lot of options when choosing a college. It was probably more than some people and less than others. My parents had already eliminated private colleges due to high tuitions. I did visit Saint Cloud State University and the University of Minnesota, Duluth and had offers to play baseball at both places. I also had an offer to go back to New Jersey and play baseball at Trenton State University. Vermilion Community College was right there in Ely, and Coach Altavilla had talked to me about playing baseball and basketball.

I got turned off about Saint Cloud when I did my campus tour with a fifth year freshman as a tour guide. Great looking girl, but not real motivated. I was excited about UMD until it hit me that Wade Stadium was their home field. I hated playing at Wade. It was cold and windy, and I had been hit in the forehead by a line drive at third base when I lost the ball in the sun and received a pretty serious concussion.

All that said, what I wanted was a good education and a place to continue playing baseball. I was officially in love with Pam, and she was a senior at Ely High School. Vermilion Community College covered it all and was affordable. Reasonable tuition and I could play baseball and basketball, keep my job at Kat's Liquor, and not have the stress of a long distance relationship.

My two years at Vermilion were great. I can't think of any instructors I didn't enjoy, and I liked all my classes. I met a lot of good people. Most of the students were from northeastern Minnesota, but a lot of my teammates on the basketball and baseball team were from out of the area.

I didn't play as much on the basketball team as I would have liked, but enjoyed playing anyway. I always looked at it as good conditioning for the baseball season. My teammates were a great bunch of guys to hang out with. We had a good mix of guys from Ely, Tower, Chisholm, Grand Rapids, Hibbing, Cook, and Floodwood. We also had guys from southern Minnesota, St. Paul, Pelican Rapids, Duluth, and Maple, Wisconsin. Our three imports were from Akron and Cleveland, Ohio. In the late 1970s, each school in our league had mostly players from their local area. It was a lot of fun to continue to play with and against players that had been teammates or rivals in high school. It is too bad, but most of the community colleges in Minnesota have gone away from that model and have expanded recruiting on the men's side of athletics to players from all over the country. The local flavor and interest has been lost for the most part. Baseball is really the only sport where you see the majority of the players from the local high schools.

In my freshman year, the state tournament was played at Golden Valley Community College. Flip Saunders, who had played for the Minnesota Gophers, was the coach at Golden Valley. He assembled a very good team from all over the state that year. Flip took full advantage of being a University of Minnesota graduate. On opening night of the tournament we played Golden Valley. Flip had the Gopher dance line there, and the team warmed up to "Sweet Georgia Brown" *a la* Bill Musselman. They even had the guy at half court spinning basketballs and entertaining the fans during warm-ups and half time just like at the Gopher's games.

While at Vermilion, I also developed a healthy distaste for Mesabi Community College in Virginia. I've continued this rivalry in my coaching career and have a lot of fun with it, some games more so than others. You win some, you lose some, but I never have a problem getting fired up to play Mesabi, and I try to instill that rivalry in my players at Hibbing Community College today.

When I started at Vermilion I knew I wanted to major in secondary education and get a coaching certification. I also wanted to get involved in whatever I could on campus. I did not know yet what I wanted to concentrate in. I was thinking English or physical education. Eventually I chose a social studies major with a psychology minor after I transferred to Bemidji State University.

I joined student senate during my first year at Vermilion. I never did that in high school. It was mostly organizing campus activities and voting on student life issues. I enjoyed it immensely, and it was good for the résumé. The shining moment in my student senate career was when Governor Rudy Perpich visited the campus. Prior to the Governor's Reception I was setting up a display table. I crawled under the table skirt to plug in a slide projector. When I crawled out from under the table I was between someone's legs. I stood up and managed to hit this guy in the crotch with the back of my head. I quickly apologized as well as I could and moved on to my next task. Later, I was standing in line with our provost, Dr. Ralph Doty, and greeting the state government dignitaries who were visiting the campus. When I was introduced to Governor Perpich, I reached out to shake his hand, and he jokingly pulled his hand back, grabbed his crotch, and said, "I believe we have already met."

The rest of the day went better. Governor Perpich and his wife approached me and asked if I had driven to school. I said yes, and he said I owed him one and asked if I would drive his daughter around Ely and show her the area for a while. I gladly said yes and felt redeemed. She turned out to be a nice girl and thought it was hilarious I had hit her dad in the crotch and didn't even realize who he was to top it off. Apparently Mrs. Perpich received a good report from her daughter and passed it on to our provost. Dr. Doty asked me to be a campus ambassador after that.

RANDOM THOUGHT NUMBER THIRTY

Many Minnesotans remember Governor Perpich. He was from Hibbing, Minnesota and every "Stupid Man's" hero. He was our last governor from northern Minnesota and was lovingly nicknamed "Governor Goofy" by many. One thing I remember him pushing for (that a lot of people considered him crazy for promoting) was super school districts or consolidated schools. He thought enrollments would eventually decline and smaller schools would have tough times with budgets. He thought students would be better served by larger school districts. Governor Perpich also thought we should run a pipeline to places like Arizona, Texas, and southern California and sell our abundant supply of fresh water in northern Minnesota to those areas. You make the call: crazy, stupid, or genius? If Minnesota voters could, I think we would gladly re-elect Rudy Perpich – but then again, we did elect Jesse Ventura.

Pam and I took another big step in our relationship that year. Late in the fall I decided to buy her a promise ring. I went to the local jewelry store and picked one out. All I could afford was a ring with a tiny fragment of a diamond, but it was from the heart. I couldn't give it to her right away. I had to stop by her house when Pam wasn't there and discuss it with her mom. This turned in to a three-day discussion, but eventually Tootsie approved. I don't remember the details, but I gave Pam the ring and she accepted. It was official. We had made a commitment to get married someday. There were some bumps along the way, but five years later, in 1982, we did get married, and thirty years later we are still married.

Besides working nights and weekends at the liquor store,

I had work-study jobs while at Vermilion. They were interesting jobs, to say the least. I started out with the best job on campus for athletes. I was one of many gym supervisors. This basically meant I could lift weights, shoot baskets, and play ping pong a few hours a day and get paid for it. After fall quarter it was determined that my grade point average was too high to keep a gym supervisor job, so I was moved to a library position. My new boss was Sue Walls, the librarian—a great lady and a very pleasant person to work for. The problem was you had to honestly log your hours and you had to work. Eventually I had two more work-study jobs added to my load. In the morning I would pick up a van and drive to the Hidden Valley ski chalet and pick up Clyde, Charlie, and Monte, the black guys on the basketball team, and drive them to school. Over the lunch hour I delivered lunches to the elementary school and took garbage to the dump.

After two years at Vermilion, I had built a work résumé showing liquor store clerk, gym supervisor, library aid, chauffeur, delivery person, and garbage man. I was definitely starting to build a future as a teacher, because who knows what I'd be doing in the summers between school years. I was preparing for anything. The idea that teachers get summers off is a myth.

During my sophomore baseball season, I was contacted by Coach Bob Montebello at Bemidji State University. He wanted me to come to Bemidji and pitch. I was excited because the Beavers had a good baseball team and Bemidji State had a well-respected secondary education program. Coach Montebello and a couple of his players came to one of our games in Hibbing. I had three hits in the first game and pitched well in the second. We did have a bench clearing scuffle in game two of the double header. Luckily that didn't sour Coach Montebello on my coming to Bemidji. A few days later, I visited Bemidji and committed to attending there and playing baseball. It was a great decision on my part.

I transferred to Bemidji for my junior and senior years. When I got there I knew I had made the right choice; BSU was a good fit for me. My new teammates were a great bunch of guys who focused on being a good baseball team. I was plugged in as the number one starting pitcher and kept that spot both years I was there.

Pam was now a sophomore at Vermilion, so this was our first year going to different schools. At some point early in the fall we decided to take a break in our relationship. This was very odd at first because we had been dating for three years. I was heartbroken at first, but had a sense that this break-up would be temporary and we would be back together in the future. The time apart was a lot easier for me. I was in Bemidji and very few people knew Pam there. Pam on the other hand was in Ely and under the scrutinizing eyes of friends and family. I was able to date and do whatever without being judged. Pam did not have all the same freedoms. I have to admit that not having a girlfriend had its perks. I was able to take advantage of what some co-eds were willing to do for you. Don't get me wrong—I was a nice guy, but there were some things you just couldn't pass on. Some girls were willing to cut hair, type papers, and do laundry for free. Hockey was king at BSU, but a baseball player could do pretty well too if you played your cards right.

Rob Simonich, a friend at Vermilion, was my roommate that first year at Bemidji, and we lived in Oak Hall on campus. Rob and I got along great, but we were not always the best match as roommates. Our daily schedules were different and Rob was a lot neater than me. I wasn't a slob but not nearly as neat as Rob. I know this bothered him. I liked living in the dorms and eating at Walnut Hall, but Rob was more of an off-campus guy. We remained friends our second year but not roommates.

As a baseball player at BSU, I had the privilege of being in the company of a great bunch of guys every day. Tough to put it into words; I do know I feel blessed to have had every one of those guys in my life for two years. We were a close-knit bunch of "Stupid Men." Four of my teammates were in my wedding: Grimmer, Eddy, Milly, and Lanny. Quick note: I was Turny and Grimmer was Grimmer because he was not a Jimmy or Grimmy!

Our baseball team had a close relationship with the hockey team. We were very supportive of each other. We always attended home hockey games and the hockey players were some of our best fans. Both teams worked hard at their craft and partied hard when the opportunity arose. Both teams were true believers in the "Beaver Way." Build it up, tear it down, and keep repeating.

As supportive as we were of the hockey team, I'll admit now we almost delivered a severe blow to their success. They had dry land training in the fall while we had fall baseball practice. About the time we were finishing fall ball, hockey finished dry land with a marathon run on the other side of Lake Bemidji. The marathon took place on a Saturday morning and baseball players were assigned by the athletic trainer to pick up hockey players, bring them back to the dorms, and watch over them while they recovered from the run. We had a strict set of instructions to follow. One of my teammates and I were assigned to Joel Otto. Nobody knew it yet, but Joel, a freshman, would go on to be one of the best players ever to play at BSU and have a successful career in the NHL with Calgary and Philadelphia. We almost changed hockey history that day. We were supposed to put Joel in an ice bath for a while and then run a warm bath and let him soak in that a little longer. We put Joel in the ice bath, gave him a beer, and went back to our room to watch a football game. Somehow, possibly because we were "Stupid Men," we lost track of who had checked on Joel last. Panicked, we ran to the bathroom to see how he was. Joel was blue, and his breathing was shallow at best, and he had only drunk half of his beer. We ran a hot shower on him and shocked him out of his stupor. He came to screaming and was not a happy guy. Lucky for us he really had no recollection of what had happened to him or how long he was in the tub. It turned out okay. Joel became a good friend, and went on to have a great college and professional career.

RANDOM THOUGHT NUMBER THIRTY ONE

When I am cremated, the last few places I want my ashes scattered are the gym at Central Lakes College in Brainerd, Minnesota, and the gym at Hibbing Community College. I want some freshman athlete or work study student to sweep me around and not know it. I also want my ashes to be tossed into the wind off the deck of the Pink Pony Bar in Gulf Shores, Alabama. My wife can decide what to do with whatever ashes are left.

Pam transferred to Bemidji State my senior year. This was good and bad. Good because Pam and I were back together again and bad because the before-mentioned perks to being a single baseball player at BSU came to an abrupt halt. I now had to do my own laundry, go to the barber, and type my own papers. Pam and I had one more short-lived break-up, which only lasted part of the fall quarter.

I proposed to Pam on Halloween night. It was at the playground on the swings by Diamond Point Park across from campus. She turned me down. She didn't say no to getting married—she just wasn't going to get engaged on Halloween night and have that as a memory. It could have also been that I was still in my warriors costume, had been drinking, and was working on a terrible mustache. I'll admit now, definitely not a memorable moment in time. Good call on Pam's part. I would have to try again later and definitely think it through a little better.

Another mistake I made that fall was playing intramural football. Coach didn't want us playing, but for the second year in a row, we did. We had baseball and hockey players form a team and called ourselves "Cool Breeze." To this day I don't know why we called our intramural football and basketball teams "Cool Breeze," but I do know we beat "Our Gang" every time we played, and we had the best jerseys in the league. I was a prime example of why coach didn't want us playing intramural football. We were in a play-off game and our center snapped the ball over my head. I dove on it and one of their linemen jumped on my back. I ended up with a broken collarbone, dislocated shoulder, and chipped shoulder socket, all on my right side. I was a right-handed pitcher. It took some serious rehabilitation to be ready to pitch in March. Eddy, my roommate and one of our outfielders, took great care of me during the first couple of weeks. In the end it all worked out. We had a good season, and I was an all-conference pitcher.

Over Christmas break, I took the opportunity to amend my misguided marriage proposal to Pam. I proposed to her at Christmas Eve mass. Pam wasn't Catholic, so I proposed to her just before I went up for communion and left her with the ring. When I came back she was crying and had the ring on. I took that as a yes, and a year and a half later we were married.

In May it was time to graduate and leave the college life behind to join the real adult world. My mom, dad, and sisters took Pam and me out to eat at Mr. Steak after the graduation ceremony. My mom asked why I had not graduated with the honor students, and I told her I could have, but I would not have been able to sit with my "STUPID" friends at the ceremony.

I left Bemidji having made a lot of good friends, cherished memories, and a good education. I was prepared for a successful teaching and coaching career. I did leave behind some unsolved mysteries though. If any of my teammates read this maybe they can help out. Why was our baseball theme song "Who is Going to Feed Those Hogs"? What did Grimmer really put in "Fat Shit"? What was in kamikazes at the Keg and Cork? Why did they close the Beaver Pond? What did Lanny see in that crazy girl that scratched his face, and why did Milly live alone?

CHAPTER THREE

CAREER

In the spring of my senior year I was lucky enough to get some interviews for teaching and coaching jobs. I was looking for a high school position teaching social studies and coaching baseball and possibly basketball or football.

My first interview was in Lake City, Minnesota. Pam went with me. Don't tell her mom, but it was the first time we spent a night in a motel together. Lake City had an opening for social studies and a head baseball coaching job. The interview went well, but I didn't get the job. They said they wanted someone older in the coaching position. The principal recommended me for jobs in Pine City and Moose Lake. I interviewed at both places and in Lake Park, Minnesota. Moose Lake and Lake Park both offered me jobs. I chose Lake Park. I would be teaching social studies for grades 7-12 and be the head boys' basketball coach and assist with volleyball. Lake Park did not have baseball. The starting salary was about $12,000, including the coaching. I was excited that my teaching and coaching career would begin in the fall of 1981. I was making the big bucks, so I was sure I would be able to send some money to Pam while she finished her senior year at BSU. Our wedding would be in June of 1982.

RANDOM THOUGHT NUMBER THIRTY TWO

My volleyball team lost a tough match to Rainy River Community College tonight, 3 sets to 2. We have been struggling all season to put wins on the board. Losing tonight put us out of a possible berth in the post-season. This is not easy to handle; we have been in the post-season six years in a row. There are no moral victories in varsity athletics, but I was proud of how our ladies here at Hibbing Community College dug in and fought hard all night. We have been looking for that effort all season. All we ever ask of our athletes is go out and play hard and smart and play that way all night. We want to win every time we go on the court. Tonight we lost, but we fought a good fight. We all should be able to sleep well tonight knowing we live for another day and there are other battles on the horizon.

Lake Park is located in western Minnesota on Highway 10 between Detroit Lakes and Moorhead. It was a great place to start my career. Lake Park is a small town with a small K-12 school. The community was full of great people that were crazy about their basketball. The superintendent, Gene Halvorson, told me I would retain my job even if we only won two basketball games all year, but those two wins would have to be over Audubon. He said even if we won the district title, which had not happened in the school's history, and we lost to Audubon, I would be out of a job. He was serious.

I moved to Lake Park a couple of weeks before school started. The first night I was in town, some kids stopped by my apartment and asked if I wanted to play basketball at open gym. I played with them every night that week. It took all week to figure out which kids were college guys and who were the high school guys I'd be coaching that winter. I was excited to learn that Darrel Pederson, Troy Olson, Jeff Kamstra, Rodney Savig, Barry Nelson, and Kurt Knutson were all going to be kids that I would be coaching. Between them and my assistant coach, Bud Ode, they made me look pretty good, and we won the school's first ever district title with an overtime win over Pelican Rapids, and yes, we did defeat Audubon twice that year.

In the fall I was assigned to be an assistant volleyball coach. I told the superintendent that I knew very little about volleyball. He said Coach Brooks would teach me. Coach Brooks was pregnant but was not due until after the season, so she would be able to mentor me all fall. We were at a tournament in Moorhead when that plan ended. Coach Brooks's water broke on the sideline. She was off to the hospital to have a baby, and I was debuting as a head volleyball coach. A patient bunch of seniors guided me through the rest of the tournament. I did develop a passion and an appreciation for volleyball that year and still love coaching the sport today.

When basketball started I was told I'd be coaching the ninth grade, junior varsity, and varsity teams by myself. The school board would try to get me an assistant coach by Christmas. Luckily for me one of our junior varsity kids got hurt one night at practice, and I had to drive him to the hospital , telling the other players to go home or call home for a ride. The board realized I needed an assistant for liability reasons if nothing else.

The school board hired Bud Ode, the best thing that could have happened to me. Bud was a sports legend in western Minnesota. He was one of the better athletes to ever come out of Lake Park, and I couldn't have been blessed with a better coaching mentor. Bud and I hit it off well and made for a good pair. He owned a gas station/store/bait shop out on the highway and he and his wife, Becky, and daughters, Jodi and Jana, were well respected in the community. I spent a lot of Saturday mornings at Bud's shop being grilled by the local hard-core basketball fans. I would drive over to Detroit Lakes to do the Coaches' Corner radio show and then stop at Bud's when I got back to town for an impromptu question/answer session.

I was the only rookie coach in the district in 1981-82. Bud did a great job helping me deal with some outstanding coaching veterans such as Rex Haugen (Pelican Rapids), Tom Critchley (Hawley), Dave Johnson (Barnesville), Dennis Anderson (Frazee), Bill Colbeck (Hillcrest), Bill Rose (Rothsay), Gordy Nichols (Ulen-Hitterdal), Chuck Schumacher (Perham), and the toughest one of them all, Blacky Variano at Dilworth. They were a great bunch of guys but very intimidating. Blacky always called me "@#&*!! Pup."

The regular season was progressing along okay, but I knew we weren't winning as many games as the local fans were expecting. At one point I realized that some of our players were wishing Jim Hann was still coaching. I was only the second basketball coach these kids had ever seen in Lake Park. Jim had been at Lake Park forever before taking the athletic director position in Ada. He was another local legend. We arrived home late one night after a loss, and I called for a team meeting. I made my first worthwhile speech of my coaching career. The speech basically boiled down to "Get over it! We are in this together, so quit looking back, because we are going to do big things before this season is over, but it is just going to be us!"

We went on to win one of the two conferences in our district, and we were seeded in to the sub-district tournament. We won the semi-final and went on to defeat Dilworth in the finals. Blacky gave me a "Nice job, you @#!* pup," for that one. We entered the district tournament as the #8 seed and opened the quarters against a very good #1 seed, Perham, at the Concordia College field house. We defeated Perham quite handily and moved on to the semi-final. I want everyone to know Blacky Variano helped me with the game plan, and I will always be thankful for his insight and wisdom. He suggested a soft 3-2 zone and it worked to perfection.

The district semis and finals were televised by channel 6, an

NBC affiliate out of Fargo, North Dakota. Red Schultz was the broadcaster. It was a big deal! We defeated Ulen-Hitterdal in the semis and went on to defeat Pelican Rapids in a packed Concordia field house to win Lake Park's first ever district championship. The party started there, moved on to a steak house in Moorhead, to a pep rally in Lake Park, and to an adult gathering at Kamstra's that lasted well into the morning, followed by a question/answer session at Bud's shop.

We lost the following week in the region semi-final to a heavily favored Staples team in a one-possession game. It was a disappointing loss, as all losses are, but it didn't seem to matter to the people of Lake Park. A billboard was put up by the municipal liquor store out on Highway 10 commemorating the school's first district title.

I did teach while I was at Lake Park: 7th grade history, 8th grade geography, 9th grade government, and psychology and economics to seniors. I also served as a yearbook advisor. The faculty was a tight-knit group. Murray Rose and I were the only new teachers and were quickly accepted by the seasoned staff. Roger Boatman, Curt Trygstad, Dave Eidechenk, and Terry Teiken wasted no time taking us under their wings. They taught us well, but we were also the target of many well-orchestrated jokes.

RANDOM THOUGHT NUMBER THIRTY THREE

In my early years of teaching, I came to believe that eighth grade girls were the most evil beings on the planet. They were just mean. They were mean to each other and especially unforgiving to eighth grade boys. Let's just call it a theory, but I still stand by it today.

Superintendent Halvorson offered me a contract to return to teach and coach again the next year. I gladly accepted.

I finished my water safety instructor certification in early June, so I could take a summer job lifeguarding and teaching swim lessons at the local pool. I also coached parks and recreation youth baseball. Pam and I were married on June 12th in Ely. Two weeks later, we moved to a new apartment in Lake Park about a block from the school.

I taught and coached in Lake Park that year. In the spring of 1983, Mr. Peninger retired at Ely high school and the head boys' basketball job opened up. It had been a great run in Lake Park, but Pam and I and our families were excited about the possibility of us coming home, especially since our daughter Lexie had been born in May. I got the job, and we moved back to Ely later in the summer.

This was it; we honestly thought we would live in Ely the rest of our lives. The teaching job was senior social problems and 11th grade history; no eighth grade girls. I was also the head boys' basketball coach and senior class advisor. I could also pick up some extra cash working at Kat's Liquor again. It was odd teaching and coaching with a staff that had been my coaches and teachers only six years ago, but we were definitely home.

The year went very well. The teaching job was great, and we made it to the district basketball championship game but lost to Orr, who went on to the state tournament after defeating Barnum in the region final. We had a bunch of tough kids who weren't expected to be that good. They were one of my favorite teams, definitely over-achievers. We were led by Ron and Mike Mavetz, John Tekavitz, Marley Kendall, and Greg Tulla. They were a hard-nosed bunch of kids who showed up to compete every day. We lost to Billy King's Orr team in the district final by three points. To this day I still think the Cook twins, who played for Orr, switched their jerseys at halftime because they were completely different players the second half.

The plan of staying in Ely the rest of our lives came to an abrupt end in the spring of 1984. Reserve Mining Company was shut down and all the new teachers were given lay-offs due to projected enrollment drops for the upcoming year. We definitely did not want to leave, but as with many teachers and miners, the search for a new job began.

I took a job at Norwood-Young America (Central High School), which was located southwest of Minneapolis. I would be teaching social studies and coaching basketball and baseball. Pam, Lexie, and I moved into an apartment in Norwood. We enjoyed our year there, but my old job in Lake Park came open again and we took that. It was great to finally be coaching baseball, but basketball was definitely second fiddle to wrestling at Central High School and there were no signs of that changing.

The four of us returned to Lake Park the summer of 1985. Yes, I said the four of us. Our son Blaine was born in April 1985.

We spent the next three years in Lake Park and lived in two different homes. I coached volleyball and basketball during that time. The third year we won the sub-district title in volleyball and lost to Glyndon-Felton in the district semi's in basketball. That spring I was contacted by Lowell Roisum and Jim Sundstrom, the principal and athletic director at Wadena high school. Whitey Aus was stepping down at Wadena and they wanted me to coach and teach there.

Pam's best friend, Jean, and her husband, Paul, were both teaching and coaching in Wadena already. Paul was making about $10,000 more a year doing pretty much the same thing I was doing in Lake Park. From a financial stand-point it was a no-brainer. Leaving Lake Park for a second time would be tough. We had close friends in Bud Ode and his wife Becky, and I had good basketball and volleyball teams returning.

We took the offer at Wadena and made the move east on Highway 10. We spent the next five years in Wadena, which later consolidated with Deer Creek. In addition to teaching social studies, I was an assistant football, assistant baseball, head boys' basketball, and head volleyball coach during my years in Wadena.

The first couple of years, I was the head basketball coach and assisted in football and baseball. I became the head volleyball coach the last three years. Our volleyball coach retired, and I told Jim Sundstrom I would take the job if they couldn't find anyone. I'm not sure if he looked for a coach after that because I was told I had the job a week before the first practice.

My coaching experience in Wadena, which consolidated with Deer Creek the third year I was there, was both interesting and rewarding. In football we set a record for consecutive losses, which has fortunately been broken since then by other schools. Baseball, however, was very successful, and I was blessed to be able to work with Dennis Kaatz, who is going into the Minnesota State High School League's Coaching Hall of Fame in 2012. We steadily improved the basketball program over the four years. The last year we finally broke through and defeated Staples but went on to lose to Pine River.

Volleyball also went very well. The first year we won a sub-district title. The next two years we won the conference, districts, and regions and made two straight state tournament appearances as Wadena-Deer Creek. The two state tournaments are by far my most precious high school coaching memories. The entire community embraced the volleyball team, and the fan support was amazing. Our success was definitely not a result of the coaching. I was lucky enough to have the opportunity to coach a great bunch of young ladies. They were an athletic group and dedicated to being successful. They were kids you looked forward to coaching every day. We were led by Rhonda Birch, who came over from Deer Creek. Rhonda is to this day the most talented athlete I've had the pleasure of coaching, male or female. She was recruited to play basketball and volleyball by Division I schools all over the country. She ended up playing basketball at North Dakota State University and playing on several national championship teams there. Rhonda may have led us, but we would have never enjoyed the success we had without the likes of Jackie Uselman, Nayda White, Jody Pearson, Hally Damm, Steph Jessop, Missy Becker, Erin Tangen, and Rhonda's little sister Shawna, just to name a few.

In 1990 I finished my master's degree in sports management and started applying for college coaching positions. In 1993 I received my first college coaching opportunity at Brainerd Community College, now Central Lakes College, in Brainerd, Minnesota. I was hired as the head men's basketball coach and would be the head baseball coach after the first year. I taught physical education and Minnesota History. I remained in Brainerd for four years. The first year, I commuted from Wadena, and we lived in Brainerd the last three years. The coaching went very well. We made two state tournament appearances in both sports.

I thoroughly enjoyed my twelve years of coaching and teaching at the high school level, but I would never go back. I will always be grateful to Al Holmes, Dennis Eastman, Jane Peterson, and Warren Mertens for breaking me in on the college level. Between Brainerd and Hibbing, I have been coaching at the college level for 19 years now and have enjoyed every day of it.

The junior college level is similar to high school in that you are teaching and coaching young men and women that are still in transitional periods in their lives and trying to move on to another level or phase. Anything I do to help their progression is what makes my job rewarding. Coaching at the NJCAA Division III level is unique in itself. Our players range in age and athletic abilities, not to mention maturity. Some are going to be recruited to another level; some will be done in one to two years, and others we lose after one semester for various reasons.

I have coached junior college players from 18 to 32-years-old. I have had players end up being everything from ministers to criminals and everything in between. They have come mostly from northern Minnesota, but I have had players from Wisconsin, Ohio, Indiana, Illinois, Michigan, Louisiana, North and South Dakota, Florida, Utah, Canada, and Poland. I have enjoyed every team I've coached and almost every young man and woman I've coached.

After coaching and teaching for four years in Brainerd, an opportunity arose to go to Hibbing Community College in Hibbing, Minnesota. Doug Schmitz was leaving his position at Hibbing to take the athletic director's position at Nashwauk-Keewatin High School. Doug called me to let me know and asked if I might be interested in coming to Hibbing. Pam and I discussed it and decided we weren't really interested. But the more we thought about it, the more interesting the idea became. Pam's family was in Ely, a little over an hour from Hibbing. My mom and sisters were in the Cities and southern Minnesota, but I also had family in the Hibbing area. Our daughter Lexie was entering ninth grade and our son Blaine was going into seventh grade. It seemed like an okay time for them to be able to move.

I interviewed for the job and was offered a contract a few days later. After more consideration, we decided to take the job and move to Hibbing. I am currently in my 15th year at Hibbing Community College. I coached the men's basketball team the first ten years, and I am in my fifth year coaching the women's team. I also coached baseball for 13 years and have been the volleyball coach since 2000.

Coaching and teaching at Hibbing has been a great ride. I have had the opportunity to work with some outstanding people and have almost all fond memories of the young men and women I have coached and taught.

In my 13 years of coaching baseball, we made four state tournament appearances. Not an easy task considering how good Itasca Community College in Grand Rapids, coached by my good friend Justin Lamppa, and Mesabi Community College, coached by another good friend, Brad Scott, have been over the years. We also made 13 spring trips. You can't play baseball in Minnesota in March, so spring trips are a must. The spring trip was always a unique adventure with every team. As much as I looked forward to going every year, it was always a relief to "Arrive Alive" back to Hibbing. We have traveled to and played in Florida, South Carolina, Tennessee, Alabama, Mississippi, Louisiana, Texas, Oklahoma, Missouri, Kansas, and Iowa.

We always played Division l and ll teams. We won very few

games against those teams, but I hope my ex-players cherish the memories created on those trips as much as I do. Some memories were created by weather: blizzards, major rainstorms, tornadoes, and on the other hand, 80 and 90 degree sunny days. Other memories were based on players excited about their first trip out of Minnesota or seeing the ocean for the first time. Girls with southern accents and (something you just don't see in Minnesota in March) girls in bikinis were always a big attraction. A few teams made it to the Louisville Slugger Plant, NCAA Hall of Fame, and the Field of Dreams movie site. We were also able to stop at several major universities and take in a baseball game and tour the campus. All totaled, we probably blew about twenty tires on vans and caught one van on fire but luckily never had any serious accidents. We probably got lost in every state we traveled in, and why not? With vans full of "Stupid Men," who was going to ask for directions? We never did run out of gas, though. I will also admit to and apologize for going the wrong way on a few one-way streets and occasionally leaving vans containing the rest of the team behind at red lights.

I will always have a deep sense of respect for the baseball teams I coached at Hibbing. Those kids handled a lot of adversity and always continued to compete. We always played very challenging schedules and played in all kinds of weather, mostly cold. One year we traveled to Council Bluffs, Iowa, to play Iowa Western Community College. As we did every year, we left about 10:00 p.m. on a Thursday night. Other years the plan had always been drive ten hours to Council Bluffs, practice, eat lunch, check in at the hotel and crash for the night, and then play double headers on Saturday and Sunday and go home. This year would be different. When we arrived, Iowa Western was taking batting practice and was ready to play. A major storm was predicted for Saturday, so they were hoping we could play right then. We got dressed, took batting practice, and played a double header after spending ten hours on the road. Don't ever think junior college baseball players are spoiled.

Like I said before, we always competed; we had fun, but we always competed. Every once in a while someone had too much fun, so we had a few 5:30 a.m. team runs on the beach, mall parking lots, up and down large hills, and along highways and roads. Nothing is more fun than watching 18-22 year-old young men running and puking early in the morning while you drink coffee and read the newspaper and talk smart. One year the softball team got to join in on the fun in Hattiesburg, Mississippi. They protested that they had been falsely accused but joined in on the run anyway.

I coached ten years of men's basketball at Hibbing, and we made it to five state tournaments. In my four years at Central Lakes and ten at Hibbing, we always tried to assemble local kids, players from the area or that had family ties to the area. Then we would sprinkle in a few kids from out of the area. The local kids had to compete hard to play and succeed in our league, and they did. I always found a sense of pride in running the 18- and 19-year-old kids from Brainerd, Hibbing, Floodwood, Crosby-Ironton, Nashwauk, Aitkin, Tower, Pierz, Cotton, etc. up against the 23- to 25-year-old players from Chicago, Detroit, Milwaukee, and Cleveland that many of our opponents were stocked with. We stepped up and won a lot of those battles. As our league began to bring in more and more players from out of the area, I became disenchanted with coaching in the league. This is when I decided to move over to the women's side and coach women's basketball.

I am in my fifth year coaching women's basketball. We have been to two region championships and are working on getting to our third regional this year. Coaching women's basketball has been a good career change. The teams in our league are made up of mostly players from the areas that surround their college. This makes for some great rivalries and fans are very supportive. The women, for the most part, are a joy to coach. They tend to put personal egos aside and focus on being a good team. They don't get hung up in personal numbers; they just want to put a good product on the court and have fun. Sometimes I wish they would be more passionate about the sport. The young women I have coached have taught me an important lesson; athletics is something we do, not who we are. Basketball is something we do; it's not who we are. I admit they have it right. Sports don't identify us; they are just a part of the mix that makes up who we are.

I have coached volleyball at Hibbing for the past 11 years. We have been very successful. It took us until the fifth year to get to the post-season. Then we rattled off six straight post-season appearances, two conference titles, one third place finish at nationals, and two region runner-ups. This past year we didn't make the post-season, but I'm confident we'll get back to that level soon.

RANDOM THOUGHT NUMBER THIRTY FOUR

I hope Anna Van Tassel, our retired athletic director, and Gerry Levos, our retired volleyball coach, are proud of how we are doing with women's basketball and volleyball. They are the ones who put Hibbing Community College women's athletics on the map. They were always passionate about what they did and ran their programs with the utmost integrity and always put the student-athlete first. I can only hope to be respected as much as these two ladies when I am done.

Minnesota women's volleyball is outstanding at all levels. I started coaching volleyball in Minnesota in 1981 and think the level of play has advanced further than any other sport, male or female. I watched high school volleyball in the 1970s. There is no comparison to how the game is played today. There were some good athletes—Sherry Hill from Ely comes to mind—but varsity teams of that era would have a hard time competing against a good freshman team today. Many of the players begin playing Junior Olympic volleyball when they are twelve and continue to play year round all the way up the line. The skill sets they develop are amazing. Several of my players have been multi-sport athletes. Considering most of the players I have coached in volleyball and basketball, I would say they are much more confident on a volleyball court.

This is my 31st year of teaching and coaching. I have coached a minimum of two sports each year and three sports for 25 of those years. Not to mention summer coaching jobs and camps. This career would never have been possible without the constant support of my wife and children. I would never want to see a list of what I may have missed while coaching. I can only hope that I have managed to be a good husband, father, and provider through it all.

My son and daughter were both athletes themselves, I hope by their choice. I did have the opportunity to coach my daughter's Junior Olympic volleyball team for a couple of years, and I hope she enjoyed that as much as I did. Lexie did choose coaching as a career path. She has been the head volleyball coach at Peru State College in Nebraska for five years now. She has done very well, and I am proud of her accomplishments. She is planning on stepping away from coaching to start a family. I hope that she is making a good choice. I am looking forward to having grandchildren, and maybe she'll return to coaching someday.

I coached my son in various youth sports and in VFW and American Legion baseball. I will always be especially thankful for the two years he played basketball and baseball at Hibbing Community College. I know I was hard on him, and we had some stressful times trying to balance the dad/coach and son/player relationship. I really enjoyed those two years, but I am glad to be just dad again. Blaine went on to Central Methodist University in Missouri, played basketball, and graduated with a degree in psychology. He dabbled in coaching for one year as a graduate assistant basketball coach at Peru State. He decided that wasn't for him and his put his psychology degree to work as a counselor for troubled juveniles in Minneapolis. He loves what he is doing and is good at it. Even a "Stupid Man" knows to be happy and proud of your son when he is doing so well, and I am.

I will never be able to thank my wife enough for all that she has endured over the years. All the time that has been devoted to practices, games, travel, camps, clinics, late night film sessions, and when I am home being tired or just distracted. She has been patient and supportive through all of it, including the gypsy lifestyle and moving our family from job to job—moves to Lake Park, Ely, and Norwood, back to Lake Park, Wadena, Brainerd, and Hibbing. Yes, I may be a "Stupid Man," as she reminds me on a fairly regular basis, but she is what brings any sense of sanity to my life.

I have an excellent assistant basketball coach, Kate Brau. Hopefully I can retire in three or four years and Kate can take over the women's basketball program. She will do a great job. I hope to retire in three to four years, but my wife and my financial advisor at Edward Jones don't seem to be on board with my retirement plans yet.

RANDOM THOUGHT NUMBER THIRTY FIVE

My wife and several lady friends and relatives are hosting their 7th annual Christmas Tea and Boutique at our Bed and Breakfast this weekend. They serve close to 300 women over a two-day period. It is a wonderful event – the women have tea and lunch and then shop the Christmas decorations that are displayed on over thirty trees throughout the house. Pam and the ladies that help her all get stressed out about it, but they have a great time, all things considered. I, on the other hand, look forward to leaving town for a basketball trip. Now that I coach women's basketball, there is no escaping the overdose of estrogen. Today, Sunday, the second day of the tea, I will try to survive and hide in the man cave in the basement and watch football and drink beer.

RANDOM THOUGHT NUMBER THIRTY SIX

This morning while watching the Today Show, something I start most weekday mornings with, I heard that the sitcom Two and a Half Men viewership ratings are up 20% in this new season without Charlie Sheen. How do the CBS executives look now? Duh, Winning!

CHAPTER FOUR

MARRIAGE AND KIDS

If you are still reading this book, thanks for sticking with it. I appreciate your support. If you are enjoying the book, please recommend it to your friends, or better yet, buy more copies and pass them on as gifts. I also want to warn you, because you might be starting to notice that there are a lot of random thoughts in this book, besides the ones that are identified as such, that right now I am planning on writing two more chapters to this book, chapter four being the second to last. This chapter and the next will probably be full of random thoughts in no particular order because, as with a large part of my life, I'm flying by the seat of my pants. It has been a great ride, though, and I hope I'm managing to convey that to you.

Pam and I first met in the fall of 1976. I was a senior in high school, and she was a junior. I know this has already been used in a song by Savage Garden—they may have stolen the idea from me—but I can honestly say I loved her before I met her. I had already noticed her the year before and knew I wanted to meet her. Despite a few bumps in the road we dated, went steady, and were engaged on Christmas Eve in 1980 and married in the summer of 1982.

The memories I have of our wedding are scattered at best. In no particular order, here are some of them. We were married on June 12, 1982, in the United Methodist Church in Ely, Minnesota, sometime in the afternoon. Pam and her mother planned a great wedding. I had nothing to do with it other than making sure my groomsmen got sized for their tuxes. A few months before the wedding, Rod, Pam's dad, had added up the total costs of the wedding and reception and offered to cut a check to us in that amount if we wanted to skip the wedding and elope.

Thursday before the wedding, I showed up in Ely after finishing my Water Safety Instructor's course in Lake Park. I had a scraped up face. Pam, my mom, and mother-in-law-to-be were not happy. Long story short, my city baseball teammates had thrown a bachelor party the weekend before and sometime during the evening I fell down a carpeted ramp at the Viking Bar in Detroit Lakes and received some very impressive rug burns on my face. Luckily, the chlorine in the pool I was in for the WSI classes had started to clear it up. A little make-up the day of the wedding helped hide what remained.

I had to shave three times the day of the wedding. Sarah, my best man's little sister, stood on a stool and did the third shave because I was too nervous. Minutes before the wedding, I stood in the back of the church with my father-in-law to be, Rod, and he asked me to take a good look at his wife. I glanced at her, and he said, "No, take a good long look. That will be your wife in 25 years. Your wife will become her. If you can picture yourself married to her in 25 years and beyond, then go for it." He pushed the back door open and also offered an escape route if I thought otherwise. Pam and I will be celebrating our 30th anniversary this summer. She has become her mother in many ways. My daughter is well on her way to becoming her mother and grandmother, and I lovingly refer to all of them as Toots, my mother-in-law's nickname, 1, 2 and 3.

My groomsmen and various wedding guests had a great time in Ely over the weekend. Several criminal incidents, mostly possible misdemeanors, were reported in the *Ely Echo* newspaper the following week. Mostly just police calls, no arrests. Grimmer?

The grooms' party was at Silver Rapid's Lodge, the reception dinner was at the community center, and the dance was at the Yugoslav Home, which was managed by my friend Mike Petrich's dad, Bernie. I don't remember the band, but Theresa Jamnick and Zups did their usual great job on all the food. There is always great food at an Ely wedding, especially if Theresa has anything to do with it.

Pam and I spent our honeymoon at Fall Lake and Prairie Portage and ran in and out of town for gift openings and food. Our friends Carla and Dean were married the next weekend. We attended that, and then we moved to Lake Park to start our married lives.

RANDOM THOUGHT NUMBER THIRTY SEVEN

I have to get this book done. I ran into Trent Janezich today, and he asked when I would be done. Trent plans to write the foreword for the book. It is three days before Christmas and my year-end deadline is quickly approaching, so hopefully I can complete the task. I have already bought Pam's Christmas present for her to return after Christmas, so that part of my to-do list is done.

I'm not sure if Pam and I really had a parenting plan, but I do remember something about waiting three years to have kids and get ourselves a little more settled first. We were married in June of 1982 and our daughter, Lexie, was born in May of 1983, so the plan obviously went by the wayside in August of 1982. If I would have hung out with the other "Stupid Men" I played baseball with, that wouldn't have happened until at least September.

Pam went into labor early in the morning. I ran up to the school—we only lived a couple of blocks away and I could run then—left a note on the principal's door, scribbled some lesson plans on the board in my classroom, and we were off to the hospital in Detroit Lakes. Lexie was born later that morning. I was convinced we had a boy when I saw Lexie's full head of black hair during the birth, but minutes later I was proven wrong. I don't have a vast anatomy education, but it was pretty obvious that Lexie was a healthy baby girl. I don't remember much about the birthing event, but I do know most of what I learned in Lamaze class went right out the window. Pam was not very cooperative and did not want to follow my breathing instructions. It left me to wonder why, back in January, we had missed most of the Super Bowl to attend one of those classes. I did gain a whole new respect for Pam and any other woman who has given birth. I don't know that I or any other man, "Stupid" or not, could endure that.

Friends from Lake Park and kids from school began arriving by the afternoon to see Lexie and bring presents. I stopped by school to drop off candy and cigars, gloating in the glow of newfound fatherhood. Our superintendent, Gene Halvorson, stood outside the school smoking one of the cigars and seeing the kids off to the buses.

Pam and Lexie were home in a couple of days. I bought Lexie a pair of sweats to come home in. Lexie was a little jaundiced, so we had to put her in the sun on a large window sill in the living room to ripen her up like a tomato. I have vivid memories of napping on the couch with Lexie on my chest. Included in the many perks I found babies to be useful for are reasons to take a nap, and a magnet for good-looking women at the mall. You take a seat on a bench and properly display a baby in a stroller and women come from all over the mall to look.

As Lexie grew older, it became obvious she was intelligent, strong willed, and loved to be bounced. I'm pretty sure that when Pam was breast feeding Lexie, they plotted that when she was older she would spend early mornings with her dad, call for her dad when she woke up during the night, and want her dad to put her to bed. This was a devious plan, but I deserved it because I slept through the breast feeding, since there was not much I could do to help other than moral support. I cherish the times I spent with Lexie when she was little—watching *Sesame Street, Romper Room,* and *Sports Center,* taking bike trips to the park, and reading books. She could recognize Doug Flutie on a magazine cover and was correcting me when I skipped parts of a book while reading to her by the time she was two. She was reading herself by four-years-old and could do a puzzle of the United States by memory of locations of states.

Most of our children's infancies are pretty much a blur when I think about it now, so my memories are special, but random. Pam would have to tell you the details of when, who, how, where, etc... One time Lexie, Pam, and I were at a restaurant in Fargo. When we were done eating, Pam went to the bathroom and left me to get Lexie ready and take her out to the car. I got her ready, threw her over my shoulder, and started toward the door, and she started kicking and screaming, "You are not my dad!" I could only hope most of the people in the restaurant had seen us come in and eat together. It turned out later that my college roommate, Ed, who had called the day before and asked to talk to Lexie, told her the man living in her house was not her dad. I still have not managed to obtain just revenge for that ill-played gag.

On another trip to Fargo (it was the place to go when we lived in Lake Park) Lexie, who was around two or three, made it out the front door of Target by herself. It was a terrifying event, and my fault, I'm sure. Pam thought maybe we should consider a Velcro child leash. I said she was too smart for that. We never did try the leash thing because on another shopping trip to Fargo I caught Lexie letting a little boy out of his leash without his dad noticing. Two "Stupid Men" duped by a three-year-old girl.

When Lexie was born I called several relatives to let them know. When I called my grandma and told her Lexie's name, she lamented, "Who would name a little girl Texie? That is not a good name for a little girl." My grandma was hard of hearing. I told her it was Lexie, short for Alexis. She was still upset about the Texie thing because nobody in our family was even from Texas.

RANDOM THOUGHT NUMBER

THIRTY EIGHT

I hope Barb Anderson still wants to do the editing on this book. I am terrible on a keyboard, and if I have any chance of getting published, someone has to straighten this mess out.

Lexie came up to school with me every time she could, mostly to give Pam a break, but it was good father/ daughter bonding time for us. If I was correcting papers I would bounce her on my foot in her infant seat. She would also get to go to open gyms and play around. My players in Ely would tie jump ropes to her walker and whip her around in circles. She loved it. She'd scream and laugh the whole time. On one occasion my mom stopped by to pick Lexie up, and she happened to come in and see the boys swinging Lexie around. She flipped out! She couldn't believe I was allowing this to go on. That ended the walker rides in the gym for that day. Remember, this is the same lady who put me, her son, into traffic on the New Jersey Turnpike to pick up sod rolls.

Lexie loved to be bounced—on a knee, a hip, or a foot. She would fall asleep that way sometimes and wake up instantly if you stopped. She also spent a lot of time in a wind-up swing we kept in the house and was very entertained, and entertaining, to watch in her *Johnny Jump Up* that we hung in doorways. At the playground her favorite rides were the swings and those one-seat plastic animals that were mounted on large springs.

Blaine was born in 1985 when Lexie was almost two years old. Pam's labor was nowhere near as urgent this time. The first time we went to the hospital in Waconia, the doctor said it was not time yet and sent us away for a while to kill some time. I think we went and walked around to some rummage sales. Eventually we went back to the hospital, and I do not remember how much longer Pam's labor went on, but I remember watching a lot of the Master's golf tournament on television.

After Blaine was born I went home to get Lexie and bring her to the hospital to see Blaine and Pam. We let the kids exchange gifts, sort of a welcoming and peace offering at the same time. At the end of visiting hours, Lexie and I stopped by the nursery again to see Blaine and the other babies; ours was the best. When we were leaving, we accidentally took a service elevator. The elevator stopped and someone wheeled in a gurney with a covered person who had died in surgery. Lexie did not know what was under the blanket, but I remember being struck with thoughts of the humbling reality of the circle of life. We had just been looking at newborn babies and minutes later we were in an elevator with a person who had left this life. When Lexie and I got home I put her to bed and then went out on the front porch and had a beer and smoked one of the "It's A Boy" cigars. When I was done I stood up and yelled out to the neighborhood and the rest of the world, "I have a son!" I was and still am the very proud father of two great kids.

Lexie loved her little brother Blaine. She was a little rough and loud with him at first, but it was obvious from early on that there was a strong bond between them. They are 28 and 26 years old now, and the bond still seems to be strong.

I was glad that Blaine took to sports right away. As he grew up we always had sports to share: football, basketball, baseball, and hockey. He liked them all. We spent a lot of time in the backyard, in parks, at fields, at rinks, and in gyms playing all of them. Blaine was also into action figures, GI Joes, Ninja Turtles, and Starting Line-Up figures. Have you ever noticed how much some of that stuff would be worth today if it would have been left in the box?

For a while, Blaine didn't pronounce his G's very well, turning them, instead, into D's. It was fun to take him to University of Minnesota games because he loved "Doldie the Dopher!" Also when Lexie's friends came over he complained about the "dirls" picking on him.

When thinking about going to Gopher games, I have another memory that comes to mind that probably only other "Stupid Men" can appreciate. When Blaine and I would go to see the Twins, Timberwolves, or any other games at a big venue, at some point in time he would have to go to the bathroom. In a big bathroom at a large venue, the urinal is usually a long trough, something like what cows would feed at. Men and boys alike stand in a row to do their business while everyone else stands ten deep in line waiting their turn. The men pull down their zippers, stand there, and pee. The young boys drop their sweats, wind pants, Zubaz, or whatever and their underwear down to their ankles and arch back to get over the front of the urinal and pee. They are not concerned with the fact they are standing there bare-assed in a public restroom. Whenever Blaine and I go to a game now he uses his zipper, but I have to ask him sometime if he misses the freedom of his Zubaz.

Blaine was always somewhat of a perfectionist. For a long time he wouldn't put his name on papers at school, he would just write "B." It turned out he didn't like how his name looked when he wrote it. Eventually he got it and started writing his name on his papers.

When Blaine was a baby he was also useful at malls. He was a woman magnet just like Lexie was, and I'm guessing any other babies are. When we visited Pam's family in Ely, her brothers discovered this use for their nephew. They would gladly take Blaine, throw some sunglasses on him, and cruise Sheridan Street. When they came back to the house we'd ask Blaine what he had been doing with his uncles, and he would respond, "Cruising chicks!"

When we moved back to Lake Park we lived in a split-level home by the edge of town. Most nights before going to bed, the kids would have diaper races around the living room, kitchen, and dining room. It was good humor and cheap entertainment, watching two kids in diapers racing around the house.

As the kids were growing up, there were some activities Pam left up to me to supervise. A lot of times she would videotape, but it was still my gig. Coloring eggs for Easter was one of these activities. Blaine was always meticulous and neat. He liked to do blue ones, or as he would say, "Dreen ones." Lexie, on the other hand, was out of control and would usually break several eggs. She just couldn't master putting the egg on the wire wand and gently lowering it into the cup. She usually just dropped it in and the dye would splash out all over the place. Lexie usually came up with a multitude of colors because she couldn't stand waiting for the eggs to finish and would move them from cup to cup. I always hid the eggs on the night before Easter while Pam hid the baskets.

Teaching the kids to ride a bike was another one of the dad jobs. With Lexie, we kept it pretty safe. Up and down the sidewalk in front of the house and in the church parking lot. With Blaine, we ventured over to the bank parking lot. Big mistake! He ran into the drive thru, hit the curb, flew off the bike and banged his face up pretty good.

Cutting down the family Christmas tree has been another activity reserved for mostly the kids and me. At first it was Lexie and me, with Blaine joining in when he got a little older. Lately it has just been Blaine and me. Pam has always requested a white pine, because she likes the long needles. She has no idea how hard it has been to come up with a white pine every year. This year she did allow Blaine and me to go to the Brandon Tree Farm and find a spruce. I remember one year in particular when Lexie was about three. Paul Weinzierl and I went to a farm in Perham and brought Lexie with us. There was a massive amount of snow that year, and Lexie was having a tough go of it trudging through the snow. Paul and I, being two resourceful "Stupid Men," used Lexie as a marker. We would stick her about chest deep in the snow next to a chosen tree while we went off and looked at others. It was working out okay until at one point we heard Lexie giggling. We came back to where we had left Lexie and found somebody's Labrador licking hot chocolate off Lexie's face. She was unable to defend herself because her arms were stuck under the snow. We rescued Lexie and decided to cut that tree and go home.

I remember the bike-riding lessons pretty well, but I especially remember the feeling of when you first let go of the back of the seat and you release them to go on their own. It is scary. All you can do is watch and hope they manage on their own okay. The first time I experienced this with Lexie was in July 1983. She was a couple of months old. I was teaching a mommy and me swimming class. Pam wanted me to bring Lexie to the class and I could be the mommy. The class was only three days long. On the third day you blow in the baby's face so they close their mouth and you take them under the water and release them. Easier said than done, but amazing to watch how naturally they take to swimming and how far they swim underwater.

If I have lost you, the point I'm getting at here is how hard it is in those moments you have to let go. Their first steps, crossing the street, riding a bike, first sleepovers, first days of school, dropping them off at the pool or tennis lessons, leaving them with a babysitter, leaving them without a babysitter, driving, first dates, and so on. And the more recent ones: leaving them at college, moving them into their own places, and watching them start new jobs. They are all proud moments, but I have struggled with every one of them. My son-in-law, Jeff, is a great guy, but I'm not going to lie. Watching my daughter get married and head back to Nebraska was tough to deal with. Now that Lexie and Blaine are off on their own and living as adults and have been for a while, I pray often that everything is going as well as it can possibly be for them. It is not like riding a bike. You cannot run alongside of them and catch them before they fall. I just hope they know how proud Pam and I are of them and how much we appreciate every time we see them or hear from them.

Pam and I will be celebrating our 30th wedding anniversary

this June. This coming fall will mark 36 years since we first started dating. If longevity has anything to do with it, I guess you can call that a successful relationship. She is still with me after 36 years, so I must be doing something right. I really don't know what it is. It can't be my income, my dancing skills, fashion sense, handyman skills, cooking skills, or all the exotic destinations I've taken her to. I feel like by now I should be full of wisdom to pass on to young couples starting out and tell them exactly how to build a happy and successful relationship and marriage. I'm just living it, and I really don't know how to explain it to anyone else. As I said at the beginning of this chapter, I loved Pam before I met her and I've known her for 36 years and still love her. She can call me a "Stupid Man" anytime she wants because I know she loves me.

From my end, I guess I'm just like a big, old dog. I'm loyal, I'm not picky about what I eat, I don't shed much, but I do require some occasional grooming. For the most part I'm mild mannered. I am not hard to entertain as long as I get let out every once in a while. I'll pretty much go anywhere you want to take me, and I don't mind walking behind you. Did I say I'm loyal? I didn't really like a leash when I was younger, and now there is not much reason to bother with one. I'm good with kids. You can leave me home by myself, and I won't mess the house up too much. I'm not that hard to please as long as I get my belly rubbed or get scratched behind the ears every once in a while. I know my arthritis makes me a little irritable at times, but I appreciate you being patient with me. Sometimes I dream of retiring to a porch by a lake and just hanging out with you. I don't know if I said this, but I'm loyal; no matter how far I stray from home, I always come back and I will love you unconditionally until the day I die. Just don't leave me first, because there isn't a porch anywhere I could be happy without you.

RANDOM THOUGHT NUMBER THIRTY NINE

I really miss the days when all the college football bowl games were played on New Year's Day and there was just the Rose, Cotton, Sugar, and Orange Bowls. I really enjoy watching college football, but now there are way too many bowl games and it takes almost a month for them to be played. They all have corporate sponsors, and they are hard to keep track of. I do have a suggestion for one more to add to the mix, though. When the polls come out at the end of the regular season it could be determined who the worst two football teams are and they could be put in a bowl game called the "Toilet Bowl." The game could be played as a preliminary to the National Championship, and the corporate sponsor could be Crane or Kohler.

RANDOM THOUGHT NUMBER FORTY

I have one more chapter to write to complete what hopefully becomes my first book. I will write it up tonight and type it up tomorrow. I will pass it on to Trent so he can write the foreword, and then Barb can do the editing so I can get out to some publishers to see what they think.

CHAPTER FIVE

COACHING: WHAT MOST PEOPLE WERE EXPECTING!

Several people know by now that I'm writing a book. Most people that have found out about it have assumed it was mostly going to be about coaching and wanted to know whether or not they were going to be mentioned in the book. I have let some people read excerpts because they have been trying to help me organize my thoughts. Everyone has had suggestions. I have ignored some and incorporated others. My goal was to keep this to my random thoughts and memories. If I was just telling stories about coaching, then my market would be limited to just coaches and ex-athletes and I'm not sure how much reading either one of those groups do. In this chapter, I will tell a few random stories from my years of coaching, again in no particular order. I knew before I was out of high school that I wanted to be a teacher and a coach. I have enjoyed every minute of my career to this point and know I will continue to do so. I have never considered either one to be a job. Teaching and especially coaching has been my passion and what brings me back to this place every day, waiting for the next story to be written. I take great pride in being called "Coach" or "Coach T."

COACH TURNBULL'S COACHING PHILOSOPHY

First I want to make you aware of my coaching philosophy, as posted on HCC's website and included in my résumé:

"My coaching philosophy is a simple one. I treat my student-athletes as people first, students second, and athletes third. In all my thoughts, words, and actions, I attempt to teach the young adults I coach to be good people first, responsible and successful students second. The last point of focus is their level of performance as athletes.

In being concerned with my student-athletes socially and academically as well as athletically and spiritually, my commitment goes well beyond the court, field, and the immediate years I spend coaching them. I realize they are adults, but I also feel that any positive guidance I can lend them is time and energy well spent.

Over the years I have experienced many successes and defeats with my players. I have always felt proud of the positive accomplishments that we have experienced in the realm of athletics. I can honestly say that my proudest moments have come when I see them graduate or I hear of their successful careers or that they have turned out to be solid, responsible citizens.

I feel winning is important, but I also feel that the truly meaningful lessons in athletics come from learning to do the everyday physical, mental, and emotional work and preparation that is necessary to position oneself for the opportunity to win. These are the lessons that are taken from participation in athletics that help us be successful people, students, employees, community, and family members. These lessons, if learned honestly, will help us for a lifetime.

In conclusion, as a coach, I am a role model, and it is not only important to tell student-athletes that this is my philosophy, but to show them in my actions—how I treat people and how I live out my daily life. My family is the most important aspect of my life, and I have always treated my teams as an extension of my family."

RANDOM THOUGHT NUMBER FORTY ONE

I said earlier in this book that Joe Paterno was one of the coaches I idolized. Since I started writing this book, the Penn State scandal broke. I can't get my head wrapped around this thing. I've read the grand jury transcript. I've followed everything in the media, for what that is worth. I know not all the facts are out yet, but what may have happened is disgusting and there is nothing that can be done or said to justify it. We as coaches are supposed to do everything in our power to protect, support, and guide our student-athletes. To do anything less is inexcusable. It sickens me to think athletics at Penn State or anywhere else may have gotten so big that this responsibility was forgotten to save the face of the institution.

KICKING THINGS

As an athlete and in my younger coaching years, I had a habit of kicking things when I was mad. A few incidents have led to me to curtail this practice of relieving stress. When I was coaching basketball, we were playing at home one night, and Staples had jumped all over us in the first half. At some point I jumped up, called a timeout, and turned and kicked the bleachers. Stupid enough to kick bleachers but this was worse. The bottom flap was up so my foot went under the bleachers and I racked up my shin on the first row.

My players at Central Lakes enjoyed watching me kick things and purposely put things in my path when they knew I was mad. One night in Willmar, we had just received a technical foul for having six players on the court. I blew a gasket and stormed down the sideline. Someone had left a water bottle in my path, so of course I kicked it. The water bottle flew straight up and hit the scoreboard, spraying its contents into the scoreboard and shorting it out. The crowd cheered and chanted, "Fuad! Fuad! Fuad!" in reference to the Minnesota Vikings kicker at that time. The maintenance guy wheeled out a mop and bucket, stopped in front of me, and said he wasn't cleaning that up. I proceeded to quickly mop the floor and eventually the scoreboard came back on and play resumed. The next day when I came to school, my players had put a Fuad Ravez poster on my office door. To this day I have my players bring a towel to the person they are substituting for so there is no confusion of who is in or out of the game.

On another night at Rainy River, we were having a rough go of it. After what I thought was probably the 50th bad call of the night, I turned away from the court, looking for something to kick. Once again my players were ahead of me and had moved the metal medical kit out past the end of the bench. Of course I kicked it. The problem was the kit was against the wall and didn't move. I broke my big toe. In extreme pain I sat on the bench. The Rainy River hockey players in the stands began to chant, "Stand up coach, stand up!"

The clincher was when I was coaching men's basketball in Hibbing. We had just blown a lead going into halftime, and my team had headed to the locker room. I waited my usual five minutes before following them in. I was still hot and stormed into the room. A bucket of orange slices was in the middle of the room, and I kicked it and started yelling. At some point as I wheeled around the room seeking eye-contact or some sense of accountability, I caught a glimpse of Bob Morgan, one of our back-up guards. Bob was covered in orange slices and peels. He didn't even flinch, but stared right back at me. I lost it and began to laugh, as did the players. Bob hadn't played in the first half, but he did start the second half. I still kick things on occasion, but I try to do it in private.

GUTSY PERFORMANCES

In the district volleyball championship when I was coaching at Wadena-Deer Creek, we were playing Bertha-Hewitt, and Jody Pearson had her nose smeared while blocking their middle hitter. We were pretty sure it was broken and the bleeding would not stop. Jody stuffed it full of tissue and gauze and begged to be put back into the match. We put her in and went on to win the districts. One week later, we defeated Minnewaska for the region title and made our first trip to state.

When I was coaching men's basketball at Hibbing, we were playing a regular season game at Vermilion. Todd Bigelow had scored 22 points in the first half. When we were leaving the locker room at the end of halftime, Todd remained sprawled out on a bench with back spasms. He informed me that he wouldn't be coming out to warm up. I told him that I'd put someone else in. He said, "No, just put me in the book, but I can't come out for the halftime warm-up." Todd came out as the horn sounded to start the second half and went on to lead us to a win over a typically tough Vermilion team by putting up another 26 points in the second half.

In a women's basketball game in the Thanksgiving Tournament at Gogebic Community College in Ironwood, Michigan, Kelly Turk split her hand wide open between the middle two fingers into her palm. She got the fingers taped together and her hand wrapped during a timeout and played very well the rest of the game. We won, and Kelly was named to the all-tournament team. We spent a few hours at the local clinic in Ironwood so Kelly could receive several stitches. She played again a week later.

The first year I was coaching women's basketball in Hibbing, we didn't have a full complement of players. I asked Karla Elgin to play. Karla was an outstanding player on our volleyball team but was not a basketball player. She told me she had played once in a co-ed church league, but the other team was not allowed to guard her because they didn't have any female players. In our second conference game we were playing Vermilion at home. We had Karla guard their all-state center. I told Karla just to put her nose on the girl's chest and put her hands in the air and "wherever she goes, you go." Karla did exactly that all night and held her to four points while scoring a couple of buckets herself.

ABUSING AND EDUCATING MY KIDS

When my children were young they spent a lot of time at practices and games. I like to think they enjoyed it. One day at football practice, Blaine was hanging around a tackling drill, got a little too close, and got kicked in the head. He was still hurting and had some cleat marks on the side of his head when we got home. Pam was not happy and said he should not be at practice anymore. We compromised. We outfitted Blaine with a football helmet, and he wore it to all practices.

One night at a home football game I was in the press box with other assistants. Pam called in a panic to a phone in the box and said someone had called the house saying they had kidnapped Blaine and were demanding a ransom. I looked down on the sideline and saw Blaine doing his ball boy job. Turned out later to be the older brother of one of Blaine's classmates playing a sick joke.

After school one day, we were practicing in the old Wadena High School gym. I had the players on the baseline, and while I was talking, someone kept pounding at the door. I sent one of the players to check, and they said nobody was there. Later in practice, the pounding was coming from the other end of the gym. This time I went and looked out the small window near the top of the door and saw nobody. When I returned to the floor, some of my players were laughing a little but offered no explanation. The pounding started again later in practice, this time by where the sound had come from originally. I went to the door and pushed it open. There were Lexie and Blaine, locked in the wire ball cart, sweating profusely. They had somehow managed to maneuver the cart around the hallway from door to door trying to get someone's attention and be let out. I let them out. None of my players admitted guilt, and to Lexie and Blaine's credit, they blamed no one.

Lexie was always running around in the gym during volleyball practices in Wadena. One day during a hitting drill, she ran across the court and got hit in the side of the head by a ball and knocked down. We never did tell Pam, but I got her a football helmet the next day and she was good to go.

After men's basketball practice one day at Central Lakes, I asked some of my players to take Blaine across the street to the apartments to watch him and let him play some Nintendo while I finished some things in my office. When I came over to pick him up, one of my baseball players brought him out of the apartment building. I asked Blaine where Willie was, and he said he was in the bedroom taking a nap with some girl. Blaine thought that was good because he got to play more Nintendo.

One year at the state baseball tournament, we got rained out for two days and had to spend a lot of time around the hotel. Blaine was with us and started getting bored. The pool was getting old and you can only make so many trips to the mall. My guys liked Blaine, but I know he was starting to get on their nerves coming in and out of their rooms. I had to make a run to the grocery store, and I asked some of them to watch Blaine for me and they begrudgingly obliged. When I came back and was walking down the hall, I could see a large pile of something down the hallway. As I got closer, I noticed it was moving. It turned out to be Blaine rolled up in a couple of bedspreads and taped and bound by athletic tape. He was not a happy guy. I distributed the groceries to each room and then set him free.

When we lived in Brainerd, one of my summer jobs was being the groundskeeper at Mills Baseball field. The Brainerd Bears, an independent minor league baseball team, played there. Blaine was a bat boy for them. A lot of times Blaine would come out to the field and shag balls during batting practice. One afternoon, one of the players that Blaine got along very well with, let's call him John, stuck around and took extra batting practice because he was in the middle of a horrendous hitting slump. That night John went 4 for 5 and hit a couple of homeruns. After the game I was driving Blaine and his friend Andy home. Blaine and Andy were about 10 years old at the time. I asked them why they thought John had hit so well that night. I was hoping to make a coaching point and have them connect the good hitting with the extra batting practice. Their response was John had got laid. It worried me what Pam or Andy's mom might think when they heard that one. Pam already was a little skeptical about Blaine being around minor league ballplayers. I asked them what getting laid meant. They said the guys said he got to bed early. I went with it. Getting to bed early and taking extra batting practice was a good thing to do if you wanted to get better.

RANDOM THOUGHT NUMBER FORTY THREE

I hope this book thing works out because otherwise I've wasted a lot of valuable office cleaning time, and my office is a mess.

TWOSOMES

Over the years I have coached and worked with thousands of individuals, but many pairs or groups come to mind in my memories. These are some I can recall.

Darrel and Kristi Pederson, Lake Park: Darrel played basketball and Kristi was a volleyball player and cheerleader. Troy and Carmen Olson, Lake Park: Troy played basketball and Carmen played volleyball and was a cheerleader. Scott and Lisa Monson, Lake Park: Scott played basketball and Lisa was a volleyball player and cheerleader.

Hans Albrecht and John Wilkowski: Bitter high school rivals, Hans was from Crosby-Ironton and John was from Aitkin; they put their differences aside and played for us at Central Lakes College. Danielle and Chris Zubich: Danielle played volleyball for me in Hibbing and later was my assistant coach; Chris played baseball and owns Range Sports here in town. They started dating on one of our spring baseball trips to Florida. Great memory for them, but I remember that trip as the time I got food poisoning and was diagnosed with rheumatoid arthritis. Sara and Dani Ysen: twin sisters that played volleyball for me the first two years I was coaching at Hibbing. Sara played two years and Dani one. Seems to me, Dani was injured coming into her freshmen year. They are still the only set of twins I have ever coached.

Three sisters, Jessica, Marisa, and Allie Haugen, from Nashwauk, Minnesota: I had the pleasure of coaching all three in volleyball at Hibbing over a six-year stretch. Jessica, who now coaches volleyball at Nashwauk-Keewatin High School, was the first. Jessica was very reserved and quiet. Marisa and Allie were progressively crazier and less reserved. All three were a pleasure to coach but very different in their own right. Dustin and Darin Pleshe: brothers on our baseball team in Hibbing—a couple of goofballs, but great kids. They have offered to visit me on a regular basis and feed me Jell-O if I end up in a nursing home.

Wayne and Nina Kangas: Wayne was a catcher on our baseball team and Nina was an All-American setter in volleyball in Hibbing. They are both living here now and working. Much to Nina's dismay, on one of our volleyball trips, Wayne called her when he was celebrating his 21st birthday and asked to talk to me. Melissa Nyberg and Matt Erickson: Weez played volleyball and basketball in Hibbing and Matt played baseball. They are both attending

UMD right now, and I'm pretty sure will get married whenever Weez tells Matt the time is right.

Josh Shain and Nick Kepler: two baseball players in Hibbing. Very dysfunctional couple, but they did know how to push each other's buttons and get the other one fired up. Their arguments were always entertaining to listen to. Cedric Burgess and Sterry Johnson: two basketball players who played in Hibbing and came to us from Columbus, Ohio. They were big factors in our success and great guys to have around. Trent Janezich and Ryan Lee: again, basketball players here at Hibbing. They came up from Fridley. Trent has family in Chisholm and had brought Ryan to the Iron Range several times over the years. Ryan is my only ex-player to break one of the sophomore rules and Trent is writing the foreword to this book. They have both since married, not each other, and Trent lives and works here in Hibbing. John Ellich and Rich Weber: this use to be a threesome but Travis McLeod broke away and married Mark Gerber's sister, Jill. I still wish Rich and Megan would have stayed the course. Chad and Justin Bessler: brothers from LaPorte, Minnesota, who played basketball and prepared for the family business by taking the Electrical Maintenance program. They helped us get to a couple of state tournaments while playing at Hibbing. Justin married Crystal Jones, who was one of my volleyball players. If I'm around long enough to recruit their kids, I'd love to get them here. They are great people and gifted athletes.

Lindsay Jacobson and Ashley Palmer: captains of our 2008 national volleyball tournament team. These two were our only sophomores and, despite being vastly different from one another, led a very talented but dysfunctional bunch of freshmen to our only national tournament appearance and a third place finish. Babe Glumack and Gary Southgate: basketball officials and baseball umpires from Hibbing. They were working when I was in high school and still are today. They do a great job and will be missed by the whole athletic community in northern Minnesota when they decide to retire.

MESSING WITH MY LIFE OR PICKING ON ME

I like picking on people just as much as the next guy, so I'm sure I deserve anything that has ever has happened. Here are a few.

The first year I was teaching in Lake Park, there were two new teachers in school, Murray Rose and me. I was coaching basketball and Murray was coaching wrestling, and we were both fresh out of college. One night, some of the male teachers took us over to some bars in Detroit Lakes. At some point in the evening they left us to contend with some supposedly hardcore bikers. Before getting beat up, Murray and I talked our way out of it, and ended up getting rides on their motorcycles to the next bar, to the surprise of our so-called mentors.

That same year at the end of the basketball season my superintendent took my assistant and me to the Cities for the state tournament as a token of appreciation for the great season we had just completed. While walking the concourse at the Civic Center, I ran into Charlie Rogers, an ex-college basketball teammate, and his entourage. Charlie was a pimp in Minneapolis and he had some of his employees with him. Charlie and I quickly caught up on old times. He did ask if we required any services he could offer. We politely turned down the offer. I'm still not sure if my superintendent was impressed or not.

I was coaching volleyball in Wadena. We had just finished defeating Detroit Lakes, and I was waiting on the bus for the players. The last player to come out to the bus, one of my captains, said that she had left her purse in the locker room. She couldn't go back to get it because the wrestling team was in there getting ready for practice. I went back in to retrieve the purse. I came in to the locker room, saw the purse, and grabbed it off the bench. When I did, what seemed like hundreds of Tampons spilled to the floor, and I knew I had been set up. I quickly picked up the Tampons and put them back in the purse. I looked around at the wrestlers, who were dumbfounded, and I said, "I hate it when that happens," and left the locker room. I brought the purse out to the bus, tossed it at the girl, and complimented her on a joke well played.

My wife and I were looking to get rid of some furniture. I asked some of my baseball and basketball players in Hibbing if they were looking for anything for their apartments. Some guys took some of the stuff and others said they didn't need anything. One day Pam and I were walking through the alley on the way to Sammy's Pizza and noticed some busted-up outdoor furniture in the dumpster. One of the chairs was one we had been missing off our front porch. Turns out the furniture in the dumpster had been discarded by some of my players who lived in an upstairs apartment. These are the same players who said they didn't need anything when I offered free furniture. The next day I called them out on it. They admitted to "borrowing" the outdoor furniture to furnish their apartment, but had no idea I lived in the neighborhood.

Over Christmas vacation we had a late-night practice. Practice was not going very well, and I kicked them out about 11:00 p.m. and told them to be back at 6:00 a.m. the next morning. I went up to my office to take care of some work and got home about 1:00 a.m. Pam was awake and not a happy camper. She said one of my basketball players, who gave his name as Joe, had called and woke her up to ask what time practice was in the morning. The next morning, I decided to address the issue I had at home. I had two Joes, so I would have to bleed it out of them. I started lecturing the team about how I sometimes have to put up with them being idiots but my wife shouldn't have to. I told them what had happened and that someone was going to have to apologize to my wife. I saw Joe Measner staring at the floor and Joe Hansen looking me right in the eye. I went after Joe Measner, but he swore it wasn't him. Joe Hansen eventually confessed, and I apologized to Joe Measner. I told Joe H. he would be stopping at my house after practice to apologize to my wife. We ended practice about 9:00 a.m. and I got home about noon for lunch and a nap.

When I got home I was greeted by Joe, who was in the living room wearing an apron and vacuuming the carpet. Pam called out to Joe and said lunch was ready. When I came in to the kitchen not only was Joe sitting in my chair, he was eating a big plate of hot leftovers from our Christmas dinner. Pam told me there was peanut butter and jelly if I wanted to make a sandwich. I made the sandwich and headed down to the basement to watch television and eat my lunch. Later, I had gone to the bathroom and when I returned there was Joe in his apron sitting in my chair messing with the remote control. I snapped and asked him, "What the hell do you think you are doing?" Joe handed me a list that Pam had given him. It was a list of chores. He was done vacuuming the house, and he had dusted furniture and washed dishes. The last thing on his list was figure out how to get the picture-in-picture to work on the television. I told him to finish it and go home. Pam sent him home with a to-go box of Christmas leftovers. After Joe left I went upstairs to talk to Pam about what had transpired. She raved about what a good kid Joe was—a little misguided, but still a good kid. I reminded her that this was the same idiot that had awakened her in the middle of the night and earlier that year had stolen outdoor furniture from our porch. She insisted all that was in the past and Joe was actually a good-hearted kid and would be fine. Pam has always been smarter than me. Joe went on to spend some time in the Navy and now lives on the East Coast with his wife and is a financial advisor as of the last time we spoke. Joe was a goofball but was one of my favorite players to coach. He always competed hard and had a knack for helping us find a way to win. Yes, he was a good kid.

Over the years I have mentioned to some players that I have a fear of dolls. It stems from something I recall in my childhood when my older cousins, Thea and Patty, locked me in a closet with a "Chatty Cathy" doll. Two of my volleyball players, Kristen and Steph, took it upon themselves one night to allow me to face my fear. It was after they had graduated, and I'm pretty sure our trainer, Julie Lange, helped them gain access to my office. I came into my office before a game one night and found it stuffed full of dolls of all sizes. Also doll heads and other parts and I believe hundreds of little molded doll faces. I still find one of those little faces in a drawer every once in a while. When I left that night after the game, I was driving home in my truck and stopped at an intersection. I looked into my rear view mirror and there was a large doll staring right back at me. It freaked me out! I drove ahead, pulled over, and threw the doll in a dumpster. Steph and Kristen are two of the most intelligent, devious, and wonderfully twisted athletes I have ever coached. If I ever do get to full retirement I hope I am still blessed with the mental capabilities to find a way to get them back.

Coaching basketball for 31 years has sometimes interfered with Valentine's Day; just ask my wife. When Blaine was a senior in high school he had a game scheduled in Proctor on Valentine's Day. I did not have a game that night, so Tom Farrel (who also had a son on the team) and I made plans to take our wives to Blackwood's for Valentine's dinner and then go and watch our sons' game. We thought we had a great plan that should make everyone happy. Trent Janezich, an ex-basketball player, called that afternoon to say he was going to be in Duluth that night and was wondering if I was going to the game. I told him we had plans for Valentine's dinner with another couple and would be at the game later and I could meet him there. Trent thought it would be a better idea to meet us for dinner. Pam and I, the Farrels, and Trent shared a cozy Valentine's date. Trent, Pam, and Barb spent the whole dinner discussing CW television shows such as *Dawson's Creek*, *Gilmore Girls*, and the *O.C.* Tom and I had nothing to offer besides money to pay the bill.

DUMPSTER DIVING

The *Hibbing Daily Tribune* runs weekly feature articles on our athletes. There are dumpsters behind the *Tribune* building that are used for the discarding of extra and old newspapers. I have always tried to find extra copies to give to my athletes. It was easier when we lived across the alley, but now we don't, so I drive by every once in a while and check. One year I had promised one of my players I would check the dumpster for some newspapers he was featured in. It had snowed hard the night before, and the alley had been plowed. I stood on a snowbank, digging through the dumpsters. Somehow while reaching into one, I fell in. Funny as it was, I was already dressed up for a game and needed to get to the gym. I climbed out, got in my truck and sped off to the gym. On the way I realized I was in extreme pain and my ribs were killing me. When I got to the gym I went to the training room and kicked everyone out except Julie, our trainer. She determined that I had probably cracked a couple of ribs and she wrapped me up so I could coach the game. I hope that kid appreciated the newspapers.

On a baseball trip to Austin, Minnesota, I went over to McDonald's for breakfast. When I returned to my room at the hotel I couldn't find my cell phone. I asked Dustin Pleshe to call my phone to see if it could be heard, but no luck. He helped me trace my steps back to McDonald's, calling my phone as we went, and still, no luck. He suggested that maybe I tossed it in the garbage at McDonald's. I put my ear to the garbage container while he called. One of the employees informed us that he had emptied that garbage recently. Dustin and I went out to the dumpsters behind the restaurant. I leaned into the dumpster and he called my phone. There it was, somewhere under a large mound of garbage. Dustin offered to climb in and did. He retrieved my phone, covered in ketchup and special sauce. I will always be indebted to him for this act of kindness. What worries me is that he claims to have recorded the whole incident on his phone, with video.

RANDOM THOUGHT NUMBER FORTY FOUR

Earlier in this book I mentioned where I would like my ashes scattered after I die. If anyone decides to conduct a funeral for me, I would like to have the following songs played in this order:

1] "Just a Gigolo" by David Lee Roth

2] "Knocking on Heaven's Door" by Bob Dylan

3] "Moon Shadow" by Cat Stevens

4] "The Original Muppet Show Theme Song" by the Muppets, I guess.

** Don't have anyone perform these songs, just play recordings. Thanks!*

PAM AT PRACTICE

Over all these years, Pam has attended more games than she probably wants to count, but she has rarely stepped in the gym during a practice. I'm sure she feels like she is intruding. Pretty much the same way I feel when I'm in the kitchen and she is preparing breakfast for our guests at the Mitchell-Tappan House Bed & Breakfast.

Pam came to the gym with the kids at Central Lakes to tell me she had returned from grocery shopping to find that our old brick garage had collapsed to the ground and had slid down the bluff to the river. Luckily, neither she and the kids nor the car were in the garage at the time.

In Hibbing, she came to summer league one night with my daughter right behind her. Lexie was late for working the scoreboard and was in tears. Pam stood there and told Lexie to tell me what had happened. Lexie, sobbing, told her story. She had pulled out of the garage in our minivan and hit a dumpster, ripping the van all the way down the side, headlight to taillight. She swore she had hit the brake; I'm pretty sure it was the gas. She had only been driving for a couple of months, so things happen I guess. There really wasn't much that could be done, so Lexie took her spot at the table and ran the scoreboard. We later became preferred customers at Kitzville Body Shop. Lexie, Blaine, and I have all done our part to keep them in business. Pam has yet to contribute.

I always appreciate it when Pam attends a game, but I really don't look forward to seeing her at a practice anytime soon. She will still have to put up with me being in the kitchen, but I'll try my best to stay out of the way.

RANDOM THOUGHT NUMBER FORTY FIVE

It is Christmas Eve 2011. I was hoping to finish writing this book today. I feel like Bob Cratchit trapped at my desk. I have a few more thoughts to organize, so I'm going to stop now and continue next week. Blaine is home and Pam, Blaine, and I are heading up to Ely in a couple of hours. We always spend Christmas in Ely; it is a tradition. Lexie and her husband, Jeff, will not be there because they are spending Christmas in Nebraska with Jeff's family. I knew this day would come sometime, but I'm not ready for Christmas without our daughter here. I know this too will pass. Pam and I are going down there for a couple of days next week. Hopefully, I can finish writing on Monday, my new deadline. I did say I was going to finish this year!

RANDOM THOUGHT NUMBER FORTY SIX

It's December 26th, and Christmas in Ely was pretty low-key. We had a good time, though. We definitely missed having Lexie home. Blaine left this morning, and Pam and I are leaving for Nebraska tomorrow, so it is time to finish writing.

ROAD TRIPS

Most of our longer trips have been spring baseball trips, but we also traveled on longer trips for basketball a couple of times. These trips are always eventful, and here are a few of my random memories from those trips.

My baseball players were upset when we checked into a hotel in Branson, Missouri. One of them asked a kid working at the desk where the girls were. The kid had no idea what he was talking about.

We were in Galveston, Texas, walking along the boardwalk back to our hotel. A bus full of college cheerleaders drove by. There was some big competition in town. When we got back to the hotel, a similar bus was in the parking lot. My baseball players were ecstatic, and they ran off to the pool area all hot and bothered. About a half hour later, I saw them gathered in the lobby all bummed out.

They had discovered the bus was full of elderly women on a mystery bus tour.

On the same trip to Galveston, we were at breakfast and some of the guys were lamenting that Rusty Bailey was the only one who had managed to get any girls interested in talking the night before on the boardwalk. His pick-up line was, "Did you know I shot a moose this winter?"

On one trip to Gulf Shores, Alabama, we had to come off the interstate because tornadoes had been spotted in the area. It was late at night and we couldn't see anything. I found a trooper at a café and asked him what we should do. Even though we were traveling in three vans, he didn't seem too concerned and thought we should go back on the interstate. We had a team meeting in the parking lot, and I explained what the plan would be. We would continue driving. If there was a problem we would pull over, get out of the vans, and lay down in the ditch. When the storm had passed, I would start calling out names and they were to call back. Ryan Endicott was upset with the plan. He wanted to know what would happen if I couldn't call out names. I said we'd go by the roster in order of their numbers. Ryan was enraged and yelled at me, saying that wasn't a plan, it was a funeral. We calmed Ryan down, got back in the vans, and arrived in Mobile about eight hours later than planned, but we arrived alive.

One year when I was coaching men's basketball in Hibbing, we were in Thunder Bay, Ontario to play a couple of exhibition games. We played in the afternoon, and I gave the guys a midnight room curfew. Everyone made it in on time. After checking rooms I went back to my room. I usually don't sleep much on the road and a lot of times I leave my door open. It paid off that night. I could hear a couple of players out in the hall planning to go back down to the bar at the hotel. I knew they would have to come by my room to pull this off. Minutes later, they ran by my room. I stepped out in the hall, yelled, and stopped them dead in their tracks. When asked where they were going, they said to get ice for their ankles. They got the idea I wasn't buying it and went back to their rooms. A few minutes later, one of them returned to my room. He wanted to go back downstairs to meet a girl. He offered to not dress for the game the next day, run, or serve any penalty he could as long as he could go back to see this girl. He was convinced he was going to get lucky for the first time in his life. I'm sure he didn't believe me, but I told him he was young and would meet plenty of girls in the future. I sent him back to his room brokenhearted. I'm pretty sure he didn't sneak back out, and I hope he has had luckier endeavors since.

Mistaken identity but very flattering: I was standing in a store in a mall in Des Moines, Iowa, and noticed a small group of women staring at me. One of them stepped forward and said, "Mr. Clooney, can I have your autograph?" I laughed and said, "You have the wrong guy." She quietly asked if I would sign her bag anyway so she could show it to her friends. They wouldn't have to know, so I obliged. As I walked out of the store, I saw my catcher sitting in the food court. When he noticed me, he yelled out, "There's George Clooney!" When I got back out to the van to wait for my players, I found a small gift bag on my seat; it was signed by some of my baseball players. In the bag was a fake driver's license from California with George Clooney's picture on it. They had bought it in a Spencer's Gift Shop.

After returning from a long volleyball trip, I was cleaning out the team bags, food cooler, and water bottle crate. I always take the leftover food in the cooler and put it in the refrigerator in the locker room. If there are any juice boxes, cheese sticks, or Go-Gurts left in the water crate, I put them in the refrigerator also. On Tuesday before practice, we were having a team meeting, and one of the girls asked who had put tampons in the refrigerator. Nobody seemed to know who had done this. I went on later to tell them they shouldn't leave food in the water crate, but that it should be put in the cooler so it doesn't spoil before we get back. I told them they had left some cheese sticks and Go-Gurts in the crate on our last trip and I had put them in the refrigerator when we got back. Turns out I had mistaken Tampons for Go-Gurts. I haven't been able to shake this story. My volleyball players and basketball players now jokingly ask for Go-Gurts when they are in need of certain feminine products.

Out of all our spring baseball trips, we were only down South once for Mardi Gras. Our home base was Biloxi, Mississippi. The first night we were in town I asked the lady at the desk what I might be able to do with these guys after practice the next couple of days. She suggested taking them to a parade in Pass Christian. We had a team meeting, and I suggested this idea to the team. They didn't want to go. Several guys said they could go to the June Jubilee parade in Hibbing or the Side Lake Parade on the 4th of July. I told them I knew the Side Lake parade was entertaining but a Mardi Gras parade would be different than either of those parades.

We practiced the next morning and went to the parade in Pass

Christian. To say the least, we all had a great time. There were thousands of people there and the parade went on for hours. We all left with a neck full of beads. Some of my players enjoyed watching me get punched by a lady who was attempting to grab some beads I had just caught. The next day, Fat Tuesday, there was another parade scheduled in Biloxi. The players offered to practice at 6:00 a.m. so we could get to the parade and find a place on the parade route. We all got an education that day. There is a difference in Mardi Gras parades. If they were rated, I would say that Pass Christian was a "G" rated parade; very family friendly. The parade in Biloxi would be at least an "R" rating, and not a place to bring young kids. I'm sure my college baseball players would choose the Biloxi parade over Pass Christian if they had it to do again.

In 2009 I was faced with a definite conflict of interest in my coaching career. My women's basketball team qualified for the Region 13B championship game. We were hosting Madison Area Community College on a Friday night. I was supposed to be leaving with my baseball team to go to Pensacola, Florida on Thursday night prior to that. We postponed the baseball trip to Florida until Friday night after the game. The players had the vans packed and waiting. I was packed to go if we lost the basketball game. Steve Rannikar, our softball coach, was packed and ready to take the baseball team to Pensacola if we won the game, because we would be going to the National Tournament the following week.

The baseball players were very supportive in the stands, and why not, since they were going to Florida either way. At halftime it seemed as though Madison was going to win easily. We weren't playing very well and it appeared Nicole Nyberg was done for the night, having suffered an ankle injury. Nicole got taped up and had a great second half. With about ten minutes to go, Kelly Hams started going off, knocking down what seemed to be every shot she took. We ended up losing to a heavily favored Madison team by three points and the game went down to us taking the last shot. Madison went on to lose to Rochester in the National Championship game the next week. My baseball players gave me one hour to absorb the loss and then were off to Pensacola around 11:00 p.m. We drove straight through and checked into our hotel around 1:00 a.m. Sunday morning. We started a doubleheader with Faulkner State at about 5:00 Sunday evening.

On most of our spring trips, we usually stayed at pretty nice hotels. Two years ago I took my last spring trip with a baseball team. Our last stop was in Meridian, Mississippi. I wasn't exactly sure where our hotel was, so we drove into Meridian and passed several nice hotels on the way through town, but none of them were ours. When we got to the edge of town we found ours. It looked okay; a little odd, though, that there was a wall all the way around the place and a wrought iron gate at the entry. I thought the neighborhood might be a little rough, so I told the players that the wall was to keep out poisonous snakes and they probably shouldn't be out walking around. We were going to be there two nights, and I was hoping we wouldn't find any trouble before leaving for home. It was raining when we checked in, and after it stopped some of the players asked if they could walk over to a nearby convenience store. I said go ahead but watch out for snakes. About a half hour later those guys stopped by my room to let me know I wouldn't have to worry about them going out anywhere anymore while we were there. A cop had pulled over and told them that it wasn't a good idea for a bunch of young white boys to be walking around the neighborhood after dark. Despite the constant sirens the next couple of nights, I don't think I have ever slept better on a road trip. My players refer to that hotel as the "Compound."

In 1995 while coaching baseball in Brainerd, we played in the state baseball tournament hosted by North Hennepin Community College at the Brooklyn Center fields. We played the first game on Saturday morning and lost 2 to 1 to Bethany Lutheran College in a game that lasted 56 minutes. Because it was beginning to rain, we started the second game against Normandale Community College right away. That game was suspended in the bottom of the first with Tim Shereck at the plate for us. It rained the rest of the day and all day Sunday. The game and Tim's at bat didn't resume until late Monday morning. Technically Tim had a 48 hour at bat. That has to be a record. Several of the teams playing in the tournament were staying at the same hotel as us.

The rain, as I said, went on for two days. The players from all the teams were getting very tired of trying to find things to do. A pool was started on Tim's at bat and someone was taking Las Vegas style bets on things like—would the next pitch be a ball or strike, would Tim get a hit, etc. I asked Tim if he was in on any of the bets. He said he was running out of money and couldn't afford to get in on the action. Funny thing was he didn't realize he had control over the outcome of half the scenarios that were being bet on. For example, he swings, or doesn't swing. Teams were also spending time in the pool area, competing in cards, and other games for money—anything to pass the time. I stopped by the pool to check on my guys, and I was stopped by security. They were looking for one of my pitchers, Derek Schmeck, but wouldn't say why. I found Derek and we went back to the pool area. Security, the hotel manager, a lawyer, and an elderly man and some of his family members were waiting for us. The elderly man had his head wrapped in a bloody towel. He explained that Derek had been playing shuffle board on the other side of the pool. Some of our guys were playing some of Itasca's players for meal money, pizza, or some other high stake kitty. Derek had missed a shot, gotten mad, and had swung his shuffle board stick. The head flew off, went over the pool and hit the elderly man in the head. He was at the hotel celebrating his 90th birthday with some family members.

Think about it, and even if you don't have the warped sense of humor I have, this was funny. The man's family didn't see it that way, and they were threatening to sue Derek. The lawyer was there to represent the hotel. The lawyer asked Derek to demonstrate what had happened, and when he did so the head of that stick also flew across the pool. As it turned out, the sticks were missing screws that were supposed to hold the heads in place. When everyone saw this, the family's attention quickly turned from Derek to the hotel manager. The lawyer said we were no longer needed and could leave.

Last year, Steve Rannikar and I took the women's basketball team to Jacksonville, Texas, for a tournament over New Year's. We drove down in minivans. It was a great trip; we stopped at the Oklahoma City Bombing Memorial on the way down. None of us had ever been there, and I think it overwhelmed all of us. We also stopped, mainly for my benefit, and toured the Oklahoma University campus in the middle of the night. Early in the morning, I did my thing and got us lost in a rough neighborhood in Dallas after going the wrong way on a couple of one way streets. Eventually we got to Jacksonville and enjoyed a few days of some fantastic weather. We attended a Baylor women's basketball game in Waco one night, despite getting lost on campus. We played two games, neither of which we had a remote chance of winning, but they were fun all the same. My team, a bunch of northern Minnesota girls, thought it was too hot in the locker room, so to the amusement of the local fans, we sat outside of the building on the steps during halftime. We celebrated New Year's Eve with the Jacksonville team and their boosters by playing board games and eating in a room above the gym. Just before midnight, we were invited to a house outside of town to take part in an old tradition. We lined up in the backyard with several other people from the school and the neighborhood and took turns ringing a large bell mounted on a pole. You rang the bell eleven times to ring in the New Year. Most of my New Year's Eves have been pretty low key and so was this, but I thought this was a heart-warming experience, and I hope my players did also. I also want the people in Jacksonville to know how much we enjoyed their hospitality.

MISCELLANEOUS

I have a few more thoughts, questions, and memories pertaining to things that have happened while coaching, but I don't know how to categorize them, so I'll just call them miscellaneous – in other words, random thoughts.

We played baseball in a lot of bad weather. One day we were taking infield before a game with Mesabi, and I was hitting fly balls to the outfield. Our centerfielder was missing everything and was not getting even remotely close to tracking down the ball. He finally yelled in that he couldn't see the ball. It wasn't snowing in the infield but it was in the outfield.

I said before that I always thought my baseball teams were tough and competed hard. There are two teams that should be singled out; both of those teams played four games in a row the final day of the regular season because the weather had been so bad during the season.

The funniest thing I ever heard one of my players say came from Breanna Chamernick, a two time All-American and Academic All-American volleyball player. We were standing in line at a McDonald's restaurant. Breanna was in the middle line – she had two teammates in line on either side of her trying to talk to her at the same time. She was obviously getting frustrated and said, "You have to talk one at a time. I am not bilingual!"

Possibly the dumbest thing I ever said to a team occurred between games two and three of a volleyball match. We had just dropped game two and not played very well, especially at the end of the game. I was all fired up. In my ranting I said, "You can't just roll over and go tits up." What I meant to convey was, you can't roll over, stop playing, and go dead. The girls looked at me in utter disbelief and began laughing. We went on to win games three and four, and the match. I delivered a sincere apology afterwards. That group has posed more than once for pictures and prepared for the picture by saying "tits up" instead of cheese.

I can remember experiencing three extremely scary moments while coaching. One was when our manager had a prolonged seizure on the sideline during a home volleyball match. Another was when we were traveling through Little Rock, Arkansas, on a baseball trip, and a lady went shooting across four lanes of traffic during rush hour to avoid a dog. All of our vans luckily swerved to avoid her. Perhaps the most frightening thing was when I stepped out of my 4th floor hotel room to find one of my players shimmying out on a wall-mounted flag pole four floors above the courtyard to retrieve his shorts that one of his teammates had thrown out there.

I have done several stupid things over my coaching career. Some turned out okay, others not so much, but I am accountable. I left the bats in Hibbing when we went on a baseball trip to Iowa and we had to borrow bats from Iowa Western. Even though we were sharing the bats, they seemed to work better for Iowa all weekend.

I turned on the heat in the drier in the laundry room and ruined a whole set of uniforms. It was just a few days before a road trip, and we had to have a rush order of new uniforms delivered to Anoka-Ramsey so we would have something to play in. I know the players didn't like the new uniforms, but what are you going to get in three days?

On one of our spring baseball trips, the dome light in the old red van, the "meat wagon" as we called it, would not shut off. The bulb was too hot to remove, and we were traveling at night so something had to be done. I told one of my players to get some tape out of the kit and tape one of my choppers over it. A couple of hours later some of the guys in the back of the van started screaming that the van was on fire. My chopper had caught fire and now the cloth ceiling was in flames. In a truly "Stupid Man" moment, I rolled down my window to let smoke out so I could see to pull over. This just fueled the fire more. The guys started throwing water, pop, and any other liquids they had at the ceiling to put out the fire. We managed to pull over, evacuate the van, and put out the fire. We didn't have to worry about the dome light not working the rest of the trip, but the van did stink of burned plastic, rubber, and cloth the rest of the trip. The van was reupholstered when we got back.

One night at the end of basketball practice in Wadena, it was time to do a puke run. These puke runs were something I feared when I was an athlete and something I will admit to using as a coach. I have never put one of my female teams through one. They are reserved for times when multiple players or the whole team has done something that requires a serious punishment. The concept is basically the team does sprints or runs until a pre-designated number of players puke. Garbage cans are set up on both baselines and watched by coaches or managers until the desired count is reached. When we were done that night, three of my players' moms and the local photographer stepped into the gym to set up for team pictures for the yearbook and local newspaper. They had all witnessed a puke run for the first time. I had forgotten about picture night. One of the moms commented that she now knew why her son came home so tired some nights and not very interested in supper.

You might think I would run out of stupid things I've done while coaching, but I have a couple more to share. It definitely doesn't finish the list, but I'll share a few more. When I was coaching at Wadena, we were playing Staples in a home basketball game. I was disputing a blocking call that had just been made by the ref, John Klinnert. John came to the sideline to let me vent my disapproval. I was unaware that his partner, Chuck Everett, was approaching me from behind. I turned away from John yelling, "That was a charge," and threw my fist the other way as an official would do to indicate a charge. I accidentally punched Chuck in the face and knocked him down. The Wadena fans went stone quiet, and the Staples fans went nuts, demanding I receive a technical foul and get tossed out of the game. John and Chuck both knew it was an accident and found it actually quite humorous. They explained to me that they were issuing a technical, but much to the dismay of the Staples fans did not toss me out. I don't see Chuck much anymore but remain good friends with John and try to give his business, JK Sports out of Fergus Falls, as many equipment orders as I can each year.

We were playing Mesabi Community College in baseball. There was one out and nobody on, a runner at third, and our pitcher, my son Blaine, was ahead in the count. The kid at bat had been tearing us up all year. I got the hair-brained idea to intentionally walk him and try to get the next kid, who hadn't had a hit all day, to ground into a double play. Blaine disagreed, arguing he could get this kid out. I should have listened to him. Instead he did as I had asked and walked the guy at bat. The next kid up got a double and Mesabi took the lead and ended up winning. My idea cost us a possible win over Mesabi, and we always enjoy any wins over Mesabi no matter what the sport.

Luckily for me, I have coached several athletes smarter than myself. I recall two occasions in particular that this became evident as players displayed acute awareness under intense duress during games. In 1986 in the basketball district semi-final, my Lake Park team was playing Glyndon-Felton. We were down to a few remaining seconds, down two scores, and had just taken our last time out. Neither I nor my coaches could figure out a way to get the ball back or stop the clock if we scored coming out of the time out. Glyndon-Felton could just hold the ball out of bounds and let the time run out. Donny Jacobs, one of our players, asked what happens if we take another time out. I said we have no more time outs. Donny said, "I know. But what if we do?" I said the time out would be granted and Glyndon would shoot technical fouls. Donny had figured it out—the clock would stop and Glyndon would have to inbound the ball again, and if they missed the free throws and we stole the inbounds and scored, the game would be tied. I would like to say it all worked; unfortunately, Glyndon hit the technical foul shots and iced the win, but Donny was right—it was our only chance.

In 2003, we were playing Itasca in a home volleyball match at Hibbing. The winner was going to the state tournament. The match went five games and almost three hours including a forty minute delay because our manager suffered a seizure on the sideline. Itasca was preparing to serve match point in game five when Brandi Slosson, our captain, requested a line-up check. She thought Itasca was out of rotation. The referees, table personnel, coaches, other players, and fans had not detected this—only Brandi. After the referees checked with the table, it was determined that Brandi was right. We got the ball back and pushed the match a couple more points before eventually losing. Again, it didn't turn out as a win, but Brandi created one more opportunity for us to win the match.

Some things have happened over the years that leave you shaking your head and wondering if that really just happened, and you have to grin and move on. We were playing at Rothsay, Minnesota in a boys' basketball game, and Donny Jacobs, possibly the smartest athlete I ever coached, was passing the ball inbounds on a key play on the baseline under our bucket. Nobody was open, so he threw the ball off the back of the head of one of the Rothsay players who had his back turned to Donny. Most guys would have thrown it off the kid's back and then stepped in to retrieve it. Donny had a better plan. The ball hit the kid in the head and went into our basket. I don't know if that should have been a bucket or an assist—we gave Donny both, and went on to win the game.

The first year I was in Hibbing, I was sitting in my office on the first day of football practice. Kurt Zuidmulder and Murray Anderson, our football coaches, came to my office and asked if I wanted to go to Vermilion Community College to pick up some players. They didn't have enough players, and Jack Gebauer at Vermilion had too many and was looking to unload some. We drove three vans to Vermilion. The three of us sat at tables in the cafeteria and interviewed any player who was interested in leaving Vermilion and coming to Hibbing. Several were willing candidates, so we packed up their stuff, loaded them into the vans, and brought them back to Hibbing. I don't know exactly how many of them came back with us, but we did fill three vans full of players and their possessions.

On Saturdays in the fall one of my jobs was to meet and greet the visiting football team and offer any assistance I could. During the game I ran the chain crew. At first, the players on my men's basketball team served as chain crew members and later I had my volleyball players do it. Before one game against Vermilion, Keith Turner, the head coach, came to me and asked for help. He led me into the bathroom to see what the problem was. One of his offensive tackles, a mountain of a kid, was stuck in one of the toilet stalls. This kid was about 6'8" tall and weighed well over 350 pounds. I found a wrench and we took off one of the walls of the stall to let him out. The kid thanked me and finished dressing for the game. During the game, Vermilion was having their way with us and this kid was killing us on both sides of the line. I kind of wished I hadn't helped get him out of the bathroom stall. At one point he stopped on the sideline to talk to me. He very politely said that one of my volleyball players was being mean to him and kept yelling at him. The kid was genuinely upset. I asked what she had said. He said she kept yelling at him to "Get back!" It was Keshia White, and she was the "Get back" girl that day. That is the person on the sideline who walks up and down the line telling all the players to get back and stay off the chains. Keshia overheard our conversation and told him if he would just do as she said, she would stop yelling at him.

Mike Rogers from Indianapolis is by far the best basketball player I have ever coached. He played for us at Central Lakes and was phenomenal; he had no business playing at a junior college. One day in Mike's sophomore year the phone in my office rang. The guy on the other end said, "This is Coach John Thompson from Georgetown University. I want to talk to you about Mike Rogers." I thought it was a friend playing a prank and I hung up. Luckily he called back and told me not to hang up this time. He explained to me that he had seen some film on Mike and wanted him to come to Georgetown and be the running mate of a guard they were recruiting out of high school. He thought they would be a good pair. Later, we found out that guard was Allen Iverson.

I also took a phone call from Clem Haskins from the University of Minnesota one day. He wanted Mike to come down and do an unofficial visit. They were waiting on a junior college guard to make a decision, and if he didn't decide to sign with the Gophers, they wanted to sign Mike. That guard was Bobby Jackson. Mike had several other Division I and II scholarship offers in my desk drawer waiting to be signed. He didn't make grades that spring and the offers went by the wayside. I don't know how they knew, but I started taking phone calls from CBA and European teams the day after spring grades came out. Mike did re-establish his academic eligibility that summer and ended up transferring to Moorhead State in Minnesota. He blew a knee and never played college ball again. A few years later Mike moved to Houston, Texas to live with an uncle and attend the University of Houston. He called one day to tell me he had kicked Clyde Drexler's butt in a noontime pick-up game and Coach Drexler had offered him a graduate assistant coaching position on his staff.

Rhonda Birch is the best female athlete I have had the pleasure to coach. She played volleyball, basketball, and softball at Wadena-Deer Creek. She led the softball team to the state tournament and is still one of the top ten career scorers in girls' basketball in Minnesota. I remember watching her put up 70+ points on Frazee one night. I got to coach Rhonda in volleyball for three years. She was All-State and led us to two state tournaments. When she came out of high school, she was recruited by Division I and II colleges all over the country for volleyball and basketball. To my knowledge, she never did any recruiting visits and decided early she was going to North Dakota State to play. She hoped to play both sports. She ended up playing just basketball and played in or started every game for four years there. She contributed greatly to four straight Division II National titles. Rhonda was always very unassuming and humble. The last I heard, she was a very successful neonatal nurse in Fargo along with raising horses near Barnesville, Minnesota.

I've always considered cheerleaders a necessary evil at basketball games. They are nice to have on the sidelines firing up the crowd, but they are too loud on the bus and take up a lot of space that could be used to make players more comfortable. One night at Fergus Falls Hillcrest Academy, we were coming down the floor on what might have been a game-winning, last-second possession. My point guard threw a pass in the direction of a wide open teammate that I'm pretty sure would have caught the pass and scored an easy lay-up for the game-winning bucket. There was no room on the baseline, so our cheerleaders were on the sideline. One of them had stepped out on the court, the pass hit her, and the ball went out of bounds. The officials called it interference and since she was one of ours, awarded the ball to Hillcrest. They inbounded one last time, covered the ball, and sealed the win. Cheerleaders: fun to watch, but you can't shoot them.

The fourth year I was coaching volleyball in Hibbing, we were a few days from leaving for a tournament in Mankato. We had one player hurt, and would be missing a couple of players that had to go to a wedding. I was worried about playing an all-day tournament with just six players. Abby Femling was a student in my power volleyball class. She was by far the best player in class and had played in high school. I asked Abby if she was interested in playing on the volleyball team and if she was able to make the trip that weekend. She agreed to join us. We had to drop her from the volleyball class and sign her up for the varsity volleyball credit to make her eligible to play. Abby practiced for one day, and we were off to Mankato. I didn't expect to play her much, but one of the other players got hurt, and she ended up playing quite a bit. She played well and continued to do so the rest of the year. Abby tore her ACL during basketball season and ended up red-shirting for volleyball the following year. She ended up returning to school for a third year and played one more year of basketball and volleyball. She was a starting defensive specialist on our first state tournament team in volleyball.

We always traveled with insurance cards on each one of our players when we were on the road, in case something happened and we had to take them to a clinic or hospital. One year we were going to Augsburg College in Minneapolis to play a men's basketball scrimmage. I did not have a card for Brandon Hammond, one of our players from Hayward, Wisconsin. The golf coach still had Brandon's card. Julie, our athletic trainer, thought it would be okay. We both agreed the odds of Brandon getting hurt were slim. During the scrimmage, Brandon dove out of bounds after a loose ball. He hit his head on a water cart and was knocked silly. There was no trainer, so EMTs were called to the gym. They came in to the gym, checked out Brandon, and decided to take him in an ambulance to a hospital right across the street.

I didn't have insurance information on Brandon, so we dug through his bag and found in his wallet what appeared to be his personal insurance card. One of the EMTs recorded the information on a chart and they left. After the scrimmage, I went over to the hospital to check on Brandon while my players showered. When I got there, I was informed he had already been released. I went back to the gym and there was no sign of Brandon. When the rest of the players were ready, we split up and started looking around the hospital and the campus for him. Not a good feeling, knowing you have a player from a small town in Wisconsin with a minor concussion wandering aimlessly around downtown Minneapolis. Eventually we found Brandon several blocks from the campus. He was fine, and we headed home. A few weeks later we took a phone call from Brandon's car insurance company. They were confused about how Brandon could have been in a car accident inside of the Augsburg gym. Apparently I had given the wrong insurance information to the EMTs that night.

Over the years we have developed a serious, but healthy, rivalry with Mesabi Community College in all sports since I've been coaching in Hibbing. We have had several t-shirts printed up, sometimes based on players' requests and others by my doing. My favorite one is a shirt we had done for women's basketball which says on the back "Friends don't let friends drink and drive, text and drive, or attend Mesabi." I take this Mesabi rivalry seriously all year long. We have done some redecorating in our gym. There used to be wood signs on the wall depicting north division teams. They were taken down and replaced with banners. I saved a few of the signs and gave them away to opposing friends that coach at those schools. I gave the Rainy River sign to Mel Millerbernd, the Brainerd sign to Dennis Eastman, the Vermilion sign to Ray Podominick and the Itasca sign to Justin Lamppa. I don't know what happened to the Fergus Falls or Northland signs, and we never had a Fond du

Lac sign. I get along with the Mesabi coaches just fine. I consider Stack, Brad, Jo Jo, and Dan all to be good friends, but I have decided to keep the Mesabi sign. I keep it in my garage, and I use it to clean fish on in the summer.

SAD MOMENTS OR TIMES YOU JUST WANT TO CRY

Receiving the word from the doctor that athletes, such as Laura Girard, Kasey Palmer, and Audra McAllister, had blown their knees and wouldn't be able to finish the season, is hard news to take whether it is one of your players or an opponent's. Also difficult is finding out one of your players is pregnant or their girlfriend is pregnant or checking semester grades and finding out you are losing players to academic eligibility rules. When you leave one school to take a job at another, I have done this myself a few times, is never easy. Walking off a baseball field knowing you probably just coached your last game, wondering why your starting point guard is quitting the team the night before you are leaving for the state tournament, or having an athlete tell you they need to leave the team for a while because a close relative has died is terrible. Seeing young men and women pour their heart and souls into an athletic event and still come up on the short end of the final score is heartbreaking. Finding out an opposing coach is resigning because they are burned-out or have been diagnosed with a terminal disease always makes you step back and evaluate what you are doing. Hearing that one of your ex-players has been arrested or something bad has happened to them is gut wrenching.

These have all been sad moments in my career, but the toughest day of all was the first year I was in Wadena. We were practicing over the holidays, and my athletic director stepped into the gym and asked to talk to me. He had to tell me that he had received word that my dad was dying and I needed to go home, pick up Pam and the kids, and get to Abbott Northwestern Hospital in Minneapolis right away. It was New Year's Eve day. My dad died after a fight with cancer early on New Year's Day in 1989.

SPECIAL MOMENTS

I have been blessed with a lot of special moments while coaching, and I hope there are still several to come before I retire. Here are a few that stand out in my mind.

Standing courtside at the Concordia College Field House watching my 1981-82 Lake Park basketball team pick up their District Championship trophy, and looking back in the stands and watching the Lake Park fans celebrating.

Sitting on the bus in Wadena with my daughter Lexie, driving through town during the send-off parade for our first state volleyball tournament trip.

Finally defeating Staples in boys' basketball, and on Senior Night at Staples to boot.

Seeing the gym at Central Lakes packed with people from Aitkin and Crosby-Ironton, there to watch Hans Albhrect and John Wilkowski play in the same starting backcourt. Hans was from Crosby and John was from Aitkin. To say they were bitter rivals in high school would be a major understatement, even though I did say that earlier.

Having a homeless person follow our team down Hennepin Avenue from the Minneapolis Community and Technical College gym to Davanni's restaurant, just to stop and tell us how much he had enjoyed watching our team play in the state tournament.

Going to church at the Methodist Church in Minneapolis with one of my Hibbing basketball teams the morning of the consolation finals of the state tournament, and watching them share conversation and cookies with old ladies after the service.

A few years ago I was asked to do an "on-the-street" interview for the *Hibbing Daily Tribune* for their "Gimee Five" column. I was asked to answer five questions. One of those questions was to name who you would choose, dead or alive, to talk to for a while. I asked if I could choose two. My interviewer, Gary Giombetti, granted me the privilege. I chose Osama Bin Laden, so I could turn him in, and John Wooden, because I have always wanted to meet Coach Wooden.

A couple of weeks later a friend, John Potter, delivered an envelope to me at school. In the envelope were a couple of autographed pictures and a note from John Wooden with a phone number and instructions to call him. John Potter knew someone who was in a coffee group with John Wooden and the article was passed on to him. I called Coach Wooden on a Monday afternoon as he had said. We talked for about an hour, to my surprise, mostly about baseball instead of basketball, and his love for the game. I did ask him what he thought was important for young men and women to know. He said it was the same thing that older men and women need to know; he said we need to listen better to what each other has to say. At the end of our conversation he said I could call him anytime I want. I told him I was going to throw away the number and I would always cherish the time I spent talking to him that day, but he didn't need to be bothered by me again. I did throw it away, and I will always cherish that conversation with John Wooden. We lost a great man when we lost John Wooden.

Coming out of a Wal-Mart outside of Memphis and finding all my baseball players standing around with their hands on the vans waiting patiently for me. They had been told by a local police officer that if he drove by and any of them were not standing with their hands on a van he would arrest them.

Assisting Tony Cossi, one of my basketball players, install our kitchen cabinets. I was his grunt for a few days. They looked great, and he deserves all the credit.

Being a Scripture reader at Andy Nelson's wedding. I haven't made it to many of my ex-players' weddings, but that was an honor I couldn't pass up.

One day at basketball practice, when Willie, one of our players, cut his head open and was lying on the floor bleeding, I knelt over Willie and was about to help him when some of my players grabbed me and told me to get the gloves. Somebody went to the training room and got rubber gloves and they tossed them to me but kept their distance. It made me wonder what the players knew about Willie that I didn't, but it was nice to know they had my best interests at heart.

Going to haunted houses with my volleyball teams and guiding them through, just to have them run by me and give me up to any guy in a scary mask carrying a chain saw that chased us from behind.

Sitting on the porch at the Androy during Trent Janezich's wedding reception with some ex-players reviewing the sophomore rules with Ryan Lee. Ryan had broken rule #3 the night before: if you are ever in jail, don't call Coach to bail you out.

Going into the last week of the 2008-2009 basketball season, we knew that eleven different things had to occur in the last week of the season in order for us to go to the state tournament. All eleven things happened and we went to state and played our way to the

Region championship by defeating Mesabi, before losing to Madison.

Watching my men's basketball team in a dog pile on the court with the student body after defeating Vermilion Community College on a last second shot at home.

Sitting on the bench in Rochester and watching our 2008 Hibbing volleyball team be presented the third place trophy after defeating Harper Community College at the National Tournament. I can't explain how good I felt watching them and realizing that was my team.

Having Jenna Zmyslony ask me what she was supposed to do when she got introduced as a starter for our first basketball game her freshman year. She hadn't started a game during high school in Barnum, Minnesota. I think Jenna has started almost every volleyball and basketball game she has played in while at Hibbing. She has done a great job and will continue to do so at the college she transfers to. Jenna has either matured late or the basketball coaches at Barnum completely missed the boat on her. I hope they are proud of her now. Jenna is a great kid and I hope that over the past two years we have managed to restore her self-confidence. It has been a joy to watch her develop so quickly in two years, on and off the court. I can only hope this continues.

Last year we went to the state basketball tournament in women's basketball. In the second round we defeated a very good Mesabi Community College team 46 to 43. I have never seen eight athletes happier than that in all my years of coaching. If that is the last big win I am ever a part of, I know I'll never forget watching the unabashed joy they celebrated with.

Coaching third base and high fiving my son Blaine as he passed by after hitting a homerun, and watching my daughter coach a volleyball match at Peru State, will always be two of my most special moments during my coaching career.

RANDOM THOUGHT NUMBER FORTY SEVEN

I'm done writing. Now I'll send this on to Trent, so he can add the foreword and to Barb, so she can do the first edit. Then I can start looking for a publisher. If there are no takers, I'll just make copies and give them to some family members and friends; maybe they'll enjoy reading my first attempt at writing a book. I'd hate to think all that valuable office-cleaning time has gone to waste. Besides, Pam and I are leaving for Nebraska tomorrow to see Lexie and Jeff.

RANDOM THOUGHT NUMBER FORTY EIGHT

Two years ago when I retired from coaching baseball, the coaches in the league presented me with a plaque and a fishing rod. The fishing rod has a very nice cherry wood handle with the words "MIKE TURNBULL THE SILVER FOX" etched in it. I now leave it up to you to decide: "STUPID MAN" or crazy like a fox?

THE END

EPILOGUE/ ACKNOWLEDGEMENTS

I am not sure what to call this part of the book; this is the first time I've written a book and I'll admit I don't read as many as I should. I do know I want to thank some people and update what has happened since finishing writing after Christmas and passing it on to Barb Anderson to edit.

Our basketball season went pretty well. We finished third in our conference and qualified for the Region 13B tournament. Unfortunately, we lost to Mesabi 45-39 in the semi-final game. Mesabi had our number this year; we lost to them three times. All were hard- played, closely contested games, but we came up short each time. We look forward to renewing the rivalry next year.

My wife and I left for vacation after the Mesabi game. It was to celebrate our upcoming 30th wedding anniversary. I hope we don't wait another thirty years to take another vacation. It was great to be gone ten days. It was spring break, but I took three vacation days to extend the trip. This is the first time in thirty-one years of teaching or coaching that I have taken vacation or sick days. I felt guilty at first, but I got over it. Pam and I have never taken a trip like this before.

Pam works very hard at running our Bed and Breakfast and really deserved an extended getaway. Our daughter, Lexie, came home and took care of the business for the week, making the trip possible. It was a great trip. We drove to Savannah and Tybee Island in Georgia, then to Charleston, South Carolina, and Asheville, North Carolina, and spent our last night in Berea, Kentucky. We saw the sights along the way and met some great people, especially Karen and Frank Kelly who own the Beach View Inn on Tybee Island. They are nice people and have established a beautiful Bed and Breakfast.

In the Charleston city market I met a lady named Ann, selling t-shirts. I bought a couple of shirts from her. Buying t-shirts is not an uncommon activity for me. I am an obsessive collector of t-shirts. I was really excited about one of these t-shirts that was developed by Ann's friends, Patricia and Terry Keener. The front of the shirt looks something like a "Life is Good" shirt but the words are "What Would My Wife Do?" You get a shirt and a rubber bracelet to go with it that also says, "What Would My Wife Do?" I believe these are based on "What Would Jesus Do?" but are designed for men to wear with their wife in mind. Check them out on www.whatwouldmywifedo.com. Hopefully Ann, Patricia, and Terry can help me sell a few books also. I really think we have some similar thoughts—please refer to RANDOM THOUGHT NUMBER SIXTEEN.

We enjoyed visiting several historic sites in Savannah and Charleston and the Biltmore Estate in Asheville. On our last night down south we stayed at the Boone Tavern Hotel on the Berea College campus in Berea, Kentucky. They are doing a great job there. If you are ever traveling south of Lexington, consider staying at the Boone Tavern. It is just a couple of miles off the interstate.

Pam is not a big fan of ocean beaches; being the born and raised northern Minnesota girl she is, she prefers freshwater lakes. I'm still pretty sure she enjoyed our time on Tybee Island; I know it was my favorite part of the trip.

When we got back to Minnesota we stopped in Minneapolis to see my mom in the hospital. She gave us all a scare and spent a couple of days in the hospital. She is okay now, but as many of you know, it is not easy seeing your parents age and decline in health. Nothing you see, read, or hear seems to be able to prepare us for this stage of life.

Pam and I have been back a couple of days now and it's back to business as usual. I'm in Minneapolis attending the Minnesota girls' state basketball tournament and recruiting, and Pam is at home in Hibbing running the Bed and Breakfast. Hopefully I can finish signing recruits for the 2012-13 basketball and volleyball seasons in the next couple of months. Pam has the Mitchell-Tappan House Bed and Breakfast running full tilt. She would love to expand the business to a second house. I trust her judgment because she is the brains of the operation, and I hope we can figure out how to make it happen.

There are a lot of people I want to thank for helping me put this book together. Some people have contributed specifically to the actual writing of this book, but I have truly lived a blessed life, and I wish I could go back to thank all the people who have come in and out of my life that made it what it has turned out to be so far. It is overwhelming when you attempt to sit down and write about the people, places, and experiences that have created the life you live and the person you have become. Writing this book has been both humbling and heartwarming, and I hope I have conveyed that sentiment.

Thanks to Barb Anderson for having the patience to work with me and edit my writing. Thanks to Aaron Reini for helping Barb with some of the editing. Also thanks to Mary Keyes, co-owner of The Howard Street Booksellers in Hibbing, for doing yet another edit.

Thanks to Trent Janezich for writing the foreword and to some of my ex-players who contributed to Trent's work.

Special thanks to my family, players, friends, and co-workers that have taken the time to read or listen to excerpts as I was writing and offer opinions and suggestions to help move my writing along.

Pam, thanks for having enough faith in me to put up with me investing the time it has taken to write and assemble this book, despite not knowing if it would ever come to fruition.

Finally, thanks to the publisher of this book for backing me, and to anyone who purchases and reads this book.

RANDOM THOUGHT NUMBER FORTY NINE

I have enjoyed my first attempt at writing a book, and I feel blessed to have the opportunity to share my thoughts with all of you! Remember I do not tweet, blog, or have a Facebook account, but I can't imagine any of these being as enjoyable as writing a book.

RANDOM THOUGHT NUMBER FIFTY

Tomorrow is St. Patrick's Day, 2012. It is supposed to be 80 degrees. The last time I checked, I'm still living in Minnesota, so this has to be a record – just saying!

Updated June 10, 2012

AFTERTHOUGHTS

51] In my lifetime the words groovy, cool, rad, bad, fly, and sick have all been used to convey the same thought.

52] Is country music taking over the music industry? Donny and Marie Osmond are no longer a little bit country and a little bit rock and roll, they are a lot country. Have you even heard of Hootie and the Blowfish since Darius Rucker went solo singing country? Today I'm planning on buying Lionel Richie's country duet CD; never saw that coming.

53] Does anyone know what a "smidge" is? My wife does. For years, she has asked me to take a smidge off or add a smidge. When we move furniture or hang pictures or mirrors she always wants to move or adjust things just a smidge up, down, left, or right.

54] A few years ago I was driving through Mississippi and passed a sign that read: HIT A WORKER $500. Most other states fine you for hitting a worker, not reward you.

55] When did people start thinking that the statement "My Bad!" fixes whatever they just screwed up?

56] Can anyone bail me out with a home remedy tip? I put a pair of khaki shorts in the wash and apparently left an ink pen in one of the pockets. The pen blew up and left ink stains in the shorts and several of my wife's favorite yellow shirts and some of my t-shirts. It also messed up the inside washer drum. My wife is not happy with me. I'd appreciate any helpful tips for removing ink stains before I invest in new shirts. I don't need to hear the obvious question of "Why didn't you check your pockets?" The deed has been done!

57] The best excuse I have heard from one of my students for not attending class so far this year has been, "I had to have my appendix removed again." This should go without saying, but it was a freshman who said it.

58] A quote that all "STUPID MEN" should give serious thought to: "A woman's guess is much more accurate than a man's certainty." - Rudyard Kipling

59] The thermos has to be one of the greatest inventions ever. If you put something hot into a thermos it keeps it hot. If you put something cold in the thermos it keeps it cold. How does the thermos know to keep it hot or cold?

60] My wife and I had been shopping for a car for her for quite a while. We looked at Lincolns and Cadillacs, among others. It is very confusing when you start trying to sort through the differences between CTXs, CRSs, CTSs, MKXs, MKSs, etc.... I'm glad I drive a pick-up truck; F-150s, Silverados, Sierras, and Rams.

61] By the time I was 53 years old, I had been to Asheville, North Carolina; Savannah, Georgia; Tybee Island, Georgia; and Maui once. I would like to go back to all of these places again before I die. What are the odds?

62] I don't text and drive; matter of fact, I don't text. I do on occasion write these "Random Thoughts" down when I am driving. I just drove by a pole building with a large sign on the side that read: "BOAT & MINI." Would Jeff Foxworthy call me a redneck because I know just by reading the sign that it is a storage building?

63] When I was much younger, I would wake-up in the morning and one part of my anatomy would be stiff. Now when I wake up that is the only part of my anatomy that is not stiff.

64] The Minnesota Twins are painful to watch on TV this year. Thank God for American Pickers, Storage Wars, Swamp People, and Frozen Planet for providing enjoyable program options to flip to.

65] How come you never see a sign that says "Dead Bait"? I'm pretty sure every place that sells "Live Bait" also sells dead bait.

66] Everyone at some time or another looks like someone else. I have drawn comparisons to George Clooney, Kent Hrbek, Jay Leno, Mark Cuban, and—the one I think is the most accurate—Pedro Gomez on ESPN. I have even signed Clooney and Hrbek's autographs for people. I find all these comparisons unfair. I wouldn't mind having a lot of the things these guys have. Money, boats, World Series ring, expensive cars, their jobs, any of it.

67] I drove from Hibbing, Minnesota to Minneapolis, Minnesota this morning. I don't know if this can happen anywhere but Minnesota. I avoided creating any new road kill, but along the way I saw deer, rabbits, a fox, and skunks alongside the road or crossing it. I also saw cows, raccoons, a moose, a horse, and several ravens. I also got to see a black bear, Canadian geese, wild turkeys, a pheasant, an old man getting his mail from a roadside mailbox, and later a state trooper executing a drug bust.

68] You can ask any of my players, past or present: I have been known to tell a few, what they would call "Stupid" jokes, along the way to pass the time when we are traveling. Whenever we drive by a pasture of cows I usually honk. I then ask my passengers, "Do you know what those cows are thinking?" Answer: I wonder who we know that drives a van. My personal favorite, I'll credit Rick Tintor for this one: you know how you always see ravens or crows in the road pecking at road kill? How come they always fly away just before you drive up on them? Answer: They have friends up in the trees watching for traffic, and just before the vehicle gets there they call out "Car! Car!"

69] It just hit me. My dad use to pull that cow joke on my sisters and me when our family traveled.

70] Have you ever noticed how a lot of rap songs start out with the artist announcing themselves by saying things like "Snoop Dog is in the house" or "It's 50 Cent, baby!" Singers like Elvis, the Beatles, Frank Sinatra, Joe Cocker, or Willie Nelson never had to do that. You know exactly who is singing as soon as you hear their voice.

71] When did it become acceptable for the receiver of phone messages, emails, text messages, letters, and notes to ignore them and assume the sender would know their answer to the inquiries was no? Is it wrong for me to think this is rude, or is this a new standard of communication?

72] Today is Sunday and I'm traveling south on I-35 in Minnesota in the morning. I'm going to take my mom to a Twin's game for Mothers' Day. I have been passed by several cars driven by what appears to be college students returning home. The cars are packed solid: laundry baskets, a TV, small fridge, a computer, a few boxes, and a hanging plant for their mom. They are probably done with final exams and stayed for one last party last night before heading home. It seems to me, I saw a lot of these same kids heading north on I-35 over Labor Day weekend on their way to college. The pack job was pretty much the same, minus the hanging plant. Now, nine months and probably about $30,000 dollars later, these kids are on their way home. I hope they had a good year of school and have either graduated or moved closer to a degree, because we all know how expensive a college education is these days.

73] I have Rheumatoid Arthritis. I am managing it with a drug regimen of Enbrel injections and Methotrexate. A few months ago I started trying Ozone injections. They are working great.

I have gone five weeks now without taking the Methotrexate. I hope this can continue, because the side effects of Methotrexate are horrendous despite the benefits of taking it. I'll admit I don't feel quite as comfortable as I did when I was taking the Methotrexate and my wife thinks the cold turkey attempt is making me crabby. I do think I'm doing pretty well, though, so I hope to stay off the Methotrexate and on occasion continue with the Ozone injections.

74] Over the years I have traveled to a lot of out of the way places just to say I did. The most unique would have to be It, Mississippi. As you travel toward It, you pass several little signs such as "It is coming," "You are getting closer to It," "It is almost here." When you arrive, you pass a sign that says, "This is It." When you leave town the sign reads, "That was It." A little way out of town, there is a sign that reads, "You missed It." I haven't been to It since 1989, but I hope It is still there. I am a proud "STUPID MAN" that can say I have been in It, through It, and have seen all of It.

75] I attended a funeral today. The lady who had passed was 77 years old; she was the mother of one of my wife Pam's friends from high school. There were a few people at the funeral that were the same age as Pam and me; a lot of those people had their parents there. Most of our parents are similar ages. I couldn't help but notice how many of us have grown to look and act like our parents. When we were in high school and our parents were pushing their forties, I don't recall any similarities. Now that we are in our fifties and our parents are in their seventies, the similarities are uncanny. Obviously we have crossed a line somewhere along the way, where our parents went in to a holding pattern and we are steadily closing the gap; doesn't seem fair.

76] If you watched the Hatfields & McCoys on the History Channel and you run into me, don't say anything about the third and final episode. My wife recorded it for me and I haven't watched it yet.

77] My wife and I are going to a wedding this weekend. The reception is being held at a winery. Two members of my "Wine Group" have been instrumental in helping me put this book together. Barb Anderson did almost all of the pre-editing, and Peter Vandelinder scanned all the pictures to a disc for me. I don't think I can buy enough wine at the winery this weekend to thank them.

78] Looking forward to this Thursday, I'm driving down to Omaha to see the College World Series again. I'm hoping the Stony Brook team does some damage. Glad there is an upper east coast team in the mix this year.

79] Today, June 12, 2012, is a big day in the life of this "STUPID MAN." First of all, Pam and I are celebrating our 30th wedding anniversary and I am signing a publishing contract with 2 Moon Press. I am a blessed man and I'm glad there are people that want to be in a committed relationship with me.

Updated June 12, 2012

COACH MIKE TURNBULL

Head Women's Volleyball & Basketball

EDUCATION:

H.S. Diploma	1977	Ely, MN
A.A. Degree	1979	Vermilion CC Ely, MN
B.S. Degree	1981	Bemidji State University Bemidji, MN
M.S.S. Degree	1990	US Sports Academy Daphne, AL

Coach Turnbull started his coaching and teaching career in 1981. He coached and taught social studies at the high school level for 12 years from 1981-93. Coaching boys' basketball, baseball, volleyball, and football. He made stops at Lake Park, Ely, Norwood-Young America and Wadena-Deer Creek, all in Minnesota. His teams won 11 conference titles, 4 district titles, and made 2 state tournament appearances.

In 1993 he went on to teach and coach at Central Lakes College in Brainerd, MN and was there 4 years from 1993-97. He coached men's basketball and baseball. His teams won one conference title and made 5 state tournament appearances.

In 1997 Coach Turnbull came to Hibbing CC, where he has coached and taught for the past 14 years. He coached men's basketball for 10 years 1997-2007 and baseball for 13 years 1997-2010. He has coached volleyball since 2000-Present and women's basketball since 2007. His teams at HCC have made 13 State tournament appearances, 6 region tournaments, won 2 conference titles, and have won one region tournament and have been to one national tournament.

Coach Turnbull is proud to have coached five All-Americans and seven Academic-All-Americans in his tenure at Hibbing CC.

Coach Turnbull and his very understanding wife of 30 years, Pam, live in Hibbing and own the Mitchell-Tappan House Bed & Breakfast. Their children, Lexie and Blaine, are both grown. Lexie is the Head Volleyball Coach at Peru State College in Peru, NE. Blaine is a juvenile councilor in Minneapolis, MN.

COACH TURNBULL'S COACHING PHILOSOPHY

My coaching philosophy is a simple one. I treat my student-athletes as people first, students second and athletes third. In all my thoughts, words, and actions, I attempt to teach the young adults I coach to be good people first, responsible & successful students second. The last point of focus is the level of performance as athletes.

In being concerned with my student-athletes socially & academically as well as athletically, my commitment goes well beyond the court, field and the immediate years I spend coaching them. I realize they are adults, but I also feel that any positive guidance I can lend them, is time and energy well spent.

Over the years I have experienced many successes and defeats with my players. I have always felt proud of the positive accomplishments that we have experienced in the realm of athletics. I can honestly say, my proudest moments have come when I see them graduate or I hear of their successful careers or that they have turned out to be solid responsible citizens.

I feel winning is important but I also feel that the truly meaningful lessons in athletics come from learning to do the everyday physical, mental, and emotional work and preparation that is necessary to position oneself for the opportunity to win. These are the lessons that are taken from participation in athletics that help us be successful people, students, employees, community, and family members. These lessons if learned honestly will help us for a lifetime.

In conclusion, as a coach I am a role model and it is not only important to tell student-athletes that this is my philosophy, but to show them in my actions; how I treat people and how I live out my daily life. My family is the most important aspect of my life and I have always treated my teams as an extension of my family.

AFTERWORD

"RANDOM THOUGHTS OF A STUPID MAN"

January 2, 2014

I am hoping that 2014 is going to be a great year. I have decided to enter into an agreement with Rivershore Books out of Minneapolis, MN to do a second printing of my first book, *Random Thoughts of a Stupid Man.*

The book was originally released in October of 2012 by 2 Moon Press out of Marshall, MI. To my limited knowledge, sales went quite well, but when it came down to the time for royalties to be paid, the publishing company mysteriously went out of business.

I have been looking for a new publisher since last spring and recently Rivershore Books came forward with an offer to republish the book. I can't explain how grateful I am to have my book back in circulation. I have had several people say they enjoyed it and several others contact me about receiving copies that I have not been able to fulfill until now.

When I originally wrote the book, I did not do so with the intent of making any money; I just wanted to share my thoughts, stories, and memories with family and friends. Because of all the positive feedback I have received, I have been convinced it is worth sharing with others.

I am thankful to Rivershore Books for giving me the opportunity to share *Random Thoughts of a Stupid Man* with you, and I hope you enjoy the read. If you do, please recommend it to others.

I have been encouraged to write a second book, which I hope will be released soon. *Did I Say That Out Loud?* [More Random Thoughts of a Stupid Man]

Mike Turnbull

AUTHOR AUTOBIOGRAPHY

I am 53 years old and my wife Pam and I have lived in Hibbing, Minnesota for the past fifteen years. I coach and teach at Hibbing Community College and Pam runs the Mitchell-Tappan House Bed & Breakfast in Hibbing. Pam and I own and live in the B&B, but she is the Innkeeper and I claim to be the Groundskeeper. Either way, she is the boss and does a great job. Come stay with us sometime.

Pam and I have been married for thirty years and have two grown children. Lexie [Baack], who lives and works in Nebraska with her husband Jeff. Our son Blaine lives in Minneapolis and works in a juvenile detention center at city hall in Minneapolis, MN.

I have taught and coached all over Minnesota for the past 31 years. I have cherished every minute of my career. I grew up the son of Jack and Patricia Turnbull and one of four siblings. I have three younger sisters, Terri, Lisa, and Stacie. My dad was a career Navy man, so we moved all over the country. He retired from the Navy in 1975 and we moved to Ely, Minnesota where I started my junior year of high school.

I received my A.A. degree from Vermilion Community College in Ely, MN in 1979, my Bachelor's degree from Bemidji State University in Bemidji, MN in 1981, and my Master's degree from the US Sports Academy in Daphne, AL in 1990.

I had never attempted to write a book before now. I had thought about it and had been encouraged to do so by friends and family members. This past year I decided to take on the project and have found it to be both a humbling and rewarding experience.

In my 53 years on this earth I cannot pretend to have anything figured out, but I do think I have a somewhat unique story to tell, and I hope it strikes a chord with those of you who read it. I have had these random thoughts for as long as I can remember, and I've managed to write a few of them down for you to consider and ponder.

I'm not absolutely sure if this is a true statement, but I'm going to throw it out there. My college roommate Ed Nordskog became a published author this past year; his book is titled "Torchered Minds" and it is about serial arsons. I haven't read it yet but I plan to. Now that I have a book in publication, here comes the part I am not completely sure about, but I think Ed and me might be the first Bemidji State University roommates to be published authors. If nothing else I'm relatively sure we are the first Beaver baseball teammates to be published. I will congratulate Ed when the time comes, but I will also warn him to not get too cocky, because he too is a "Stupid Man."

I have always taken pride in being referred to as "Coach," second to my favorite titles as "Husband" and "Dad." I never dreamed I would ever see "Author" in front of my name. I can only hope this might help me gain entry to the "Stupid Man" club, if and when I get to heaven.

Random Thoughts of a Stupid Man
Mike Turnbull, June 5, 2012

RIVERSHORE BOOKS

www.rivershorebooks.com
info@rivershorebooks.com
www.facebook.com/rivershore.books
www.twitter.com/rivershorebooks
blog.rivershorebooks.com
forum.rivershorebooks.com

www.ingramcontent.com/pod-product-compliance
Lightning Source LLC
LaVergne TN
LVHW051236080426
835513LV00016B/1627

* 9 7 8 0 6 1 5 9 7 2 3 9 8 *